NORTH TEXAS BEER

NORTH TEXAS BEER

A Full-Bodied History of Brewing in Dallas, Fort Worth and Beyond

Paul Hightower & Brian L. Brown

AMERICAN PALATE

Published by American Palate
A Division of The History Press
Charleston, SC 29403
www.historypress.net

Copyright © 2014 by Paul Hightower and Brian L. Brown
All rights reserved

Front Cover: Dallas skyline at night. *Photo by Matt Pasant.*
Back Cover: Unopened Reinheitsgebot bottles. *Collection of Franconia Brewing Company.*
Pride of Texas Pale Ale. *Courtesy of Rahr & Sons Brewing Company.*
Employees of the Superior Brewing Company. *From the collection of Barbara Lamsens.*

First published 2014

ISBN 978-1-5402-0992-4

Library of Congress CIP data applied for.

Notice: The information in this book is true and complete to the best of our knowledge. It is offered without guarantee on the part of the authors or The History Press. The authors and The History Press disclaim all liability in connection with the use of this book.

All rights reserved. No part of this book may be reproduced or transmitted in any form whatsoever without prior written permission from the publisher except in the case of brief quotations embodied in critical articles and reviews.

"I would never think of making fine beer in this country."
—*Adolphus Busch, interview with* Dallas Morning News, *1892*

CONTENTS

Preface	9
Acknowledgements	11
Introduction	13
1. The Beginnings of Beer in North Texas (1839–1870)	17
2. Times of Transition (1872–1881)	25
3. Brewing on an Industrial Scale (1884–1893)	33
4. Anti-Trust and Adolphus Busch (1892–1909)	43
5. Texas Temperance and Local Option (1837–1882)	53
6. Onward to Prohibition (1887–1919)	59
7. Repeal and Rebirth (1920–1938)	69
8. Dallas in the Post-Prohibition Era (1934–1941)	75
9. North Texas During the War Years (1941–1951)	81
10. Miller Brewing of Fort Worth (1963–1990)	87
11. The Birth of Texas Microbrewing (1982–1990)	93
12. Texas Legalizes Brewpubs (1993–2001)	101
13. Rebuilding for Today's Craft Beer (2004–2010)	113
14. Modern Craft Brewing (2011–Present)	129
15. A Still-Evolving History (2013–Onward)	147
Appendix A: Chronology	155
Appendix B: North Texas Craft Beer Resources	165
Bibliography	175
Index	185
About the Authors	191

PREFACE

North Texas is an area with a singular history. It is not a region of great inherent resources, although areas of valuable resources can be found within a day's drive. It is not a region of great natural beauty, situated on the plains hundreds of miles from coasts or mountains. It is not a seat of any government offices at the federal or even state level, nor does it hold a strategic location for political, military or historical purposes.

North Texas—and throughout this work, "Dallas" is shorthand for the Dallas/Fort Worth/Denton greater metro area—can be summed up with one word: commerce. This is an area that has prospered through no other means than robust trade, revenue and technology with sales, money and management thereof. As such, it is a unique urban area within the state of Texas in that the cities hold no natural advantage over each other. International corporations are just as likely to headquarter in the suburbs as they are in downtown Dallas. Instead of being dominated by comparatively massive cities like Houston, Austin or San Antonio, the Metroplex is an assemblage of cities large and small, each working together in this regional economy.

Thus, when trying to document the brewing history of North Texas, one must spread the focus over the entire region, as one adjoining city can work just as equally for most purposes as any other. People often live, work, play and shop in completely different cities, and municipal borders mean less and less each year. Dallas-based Lakewood Brewing chose a location in Garland just miles over the city limit. Denton-based Independent Ale Works is located in nearby Krum because that location worked better for it. And with current growth trends, Fort Worth is projected to be larger than Dallas proper by 2030.

We will use the terms "Dallas-area," "Dallas/Fort Worth," "DFW" and "Metroplex" as synonymous with the North Texas area, which actually has a formal definition. For the purposes of our history here of North Texas beer, we have included brewing operations within North Texas as defined by the North Central Texas Council of Governments (NCTCOG). This area includes the sixteen counties of Collin, Dallas, Denton, Ellis, Erath, Hood, Hunt, Johnson, Kaufman, Navarro, Palo Pinto, Parker, Rockwall, Somervell, Tarrant and Wise. For areas much farther outside these counties, the subject clearly belongs to another work for an adjacent region.

At the time of this writing in 2014, brewing operations in the entire state of Texas are experiencing tremendous growth and flux, and no doubt, this work will be incorrect and incomplete almost as soon as it is published. However, we have tried to begin the documentation for beer in Dallas, Fort Worth and the surrounding cities and hope it can be a fun and informative reference to be built upon in years to come.

ACKNOWLEDGEMENTS

There are a great many people to thank for making this book possible, not the least of whom are the brewers and business owners behind today's North Texas breweries and craft beer retailers. We would also like to thank the amateur and professional photographers, as well as the various media outlets that willingly donated images for use on this project. Most of the names associated with these two groups are credited either in the narrative or alongside the material they provided. Beyond that would be a long list of friends, family members, loyal readers and innumerable others who make up what we know as the North Texas craft beer community.

A few of these individuals are noted here as well as those who contributed time and effort in response to requests for interviews and archival searches that have proved invaluable to this work. Also included are fellow writers who in some instances have provided coverage of the local beer scene for decades. A great deal of their work served as a vital reference for much of the modern-day history in later chapters.

Thank you to Bev Blackwood, the Brown family, Burleson County District Clerk, Randy Carlson, Dallas Convention and Visitors Bureau, Dallas Historical Society, Randall Erwin, Chris Graves, Teresa Gubbins, Johnson County District Clerk, Barbara Lamsens, Mike Nichols, Elisabeth Pope, Joe Schepps, Barry Shlachter, the Special Collections Department at the University of Texas at Arlington, John Stuart, the Texas/Dallas History and Archives Division at the Dallas Public Library, Christen Thompson and The History Press and Don and Mary Thompson.

INTRODUCTION

A study of North Texas brewing history does not begin with a tour of an abandoned brewery in one of the area's two largest downtowns. Unfortunately, other than the rare piece of breweriana, not much remains from the bygone days of Dallas or Fort Worth beer. Whether it was an old brewery or cold storage facility, the most prominent industrial buildings from the region's past went the way of the wrecking ball long ago.

Instead, those wishing to learn more about who and what has gone before with regard to North Texas beer are left to sort through old newspapers, industry journals, city directories and various works of locally focused nonfiction. The historical record in this area is patchy, leaving the writer and historian to piece together what is sometimes the slightest bit of information into something that resembles a story.

For North Texas, that story encompasses nearly 160 years, reaching back to 1857, when the first brewery was established in Dallas. Within it are common threads like day-to-day dealings with alcohol legislation (specifically, local option) and the seemingly modern-day rallying cry of "drink local." Words resembling the latter have actually echoed across North Texas history as small brewers have been going up against "big beer" and urged consumers to support their local brewery almost from the beginning. It started as far back as 1873 in Dallas when fresh, locally brewed beer was being touted over "foreign" products shipped by wagon or train, with phrases like "patronize home industry" being a commonplace call-to-arms.

Introduction

Before that could happen, the area's early pioneers would have to set foot on the lands that would become Dallas and Fort Worth. They would have to deal with the struggles of building towns and cities out of nothing on the isolated plains of North Texas. Ask a local craft brewer today and they might tell you a similar tale about their own journey and how the local industry has risen up from what some once called a "craft beer wasteland." Whether it was passion, perseverance or both, the pioneers of the past found their way, as North Texas is now among the largest metropolitan areas in the United States. It remains to be seen if the area's craft beer pioneers will be able to find their way as well, such that one day the region might be considered among the top craft beer destinations in the country.

Entering 2014, the North Texas region has experienced two years of unprecedented growth in the local craft beer industry. Looking inside the numbers, on average, a production brewery has opened roughly every six weeks since November 2011. The still-continuing trend has spurred talk of market saturation, with many people openly wondering when the "craft beer bubble" might burst. Considering those breweries and brewpubs on the verge of opening and others known to be in development, the idea that close to fifty brewing operations might exist in the very near future will do nothing the quell the conversation.

If one thing is working in the industry's favor, it is that the bulk of North Texas still represents an untapped market. Even with over two dozen active brewing operations in 2014, devoted craft beer drinkers only make up a very small part of the nearly seven million residents who call the Metroplex area home. The reality is that the vast majority of the local population has yet to embrace craft beer, and most, if not all, new breweries appear to recognize this when choosing styles for their opening-day portfolios.

Another positive is the ongoing change in the beer-drinking culture. No longer are the Ginger Man and Flying Saucer the only places in town to enjoy a craft beer outside the comfort of your own home. More and more pubs and restaurants are opening and making craft beer the focal point of their business. In fact, the sheer number of beers being produced in North Texas makes it possible for some establishments to offer only North Texas brews on tap without sacrificing variety for differing tastes.

Consumers are turning out for events as well. Beer dinners regularly attract industry figures from both local and national breweries, and Saturday brewery tours have become a regular stop for many. Large-scale festivals are also flourishing thanks to the efforts of those behind over a half dozen annual gatherings. Then there is North Texas Beer Week, a multi-day celebration,

Introduction

which in just three years has had the number of events associated with it increase over 200 percent.

A solid foundation has been put in place for local brewing that should continue to help build and support the craft beer scene in North Texas. Certainly, as more and more breweries open, there will be issues with tap space in pubs and shelf space in retail locations, but as long as local breweries make good beer, one must believe there will be more than enough thirsty North Texans willing to drink it.

1
THE BEGINNINGS OF BEER IN NORTH TEXAS (1839–1870)

Dallas got its start after John Neely Bryan staked his claim to lands at the crossroads of two trails near the Trinity River in 1839. He had designs on a trading post, but after settling his affairs at his former home in Arkansas, he returned to find the local Indian tribes driven away by raids carried out by the Republic of Texas to reduce tensions in the area. With the loss of potential trading partners, he focused instead on building a town.

Bryan established the settlement in November 1841, initially struggling to attract settlers, though he managed to convince the legislature to recognize Dallas County in 1846. Residents voted the town as the permanent county seat in 1850, but only 350 people called Dallas home by the time it was incorporated as a city in 1856. Despite the low number of residents, signs of commerce had started to appear. The town's first newspaper, the *Dallas Herald*, went to press in 1849, while other citizens opened general stores, hotels, blacksmiths, brickyards and a sawmill. You could even get a shot of whiskey as early as 1846, when Adam Haught opened the town's first saloon, but it would be 1857 before someone would establish a brewery.

Dallas's first brewer was a pioneer but not in the sense that he traveled to Texas, marked off a spot and started making beer. Jean Monduel came with scores of others from France, Switzerland and Belgium to find an ideal existence along the western bank of the Trinity River. It was 1855, and they were led by Victor Considerant, a French political activist who drew inspiration from the utopian teachings of countryman Francois Charles Fourier.

The people of La Reunion—as the resulting colony would be called—were the cultured sort, made up entirely of artisans and craftsmen. They counted no farmers among their ranks, and all it took was a long drought and a plague of grasshoppers to ruin their crops. Factor in poor management from their leader and the colonists' yearning for freedoms offered by the pioneer lifestyle, and La Reunion's failure would seem to have been predestined from the start.

After the settlement disbanded in January 1857, colonists either returned to their previous homes or relocated to other communities. Jean Monduel was among those who crossed the Trinity as he moved with his wife and daughter to settle east of the river. Born in Paris, he once held an apprenticeship at a distillery there before serving in the French army. After a tour of duty, he returned to his former profession prior to joining a group of colonists and sailing for America in 1855. Monduel was a winemaker while at La Reunion, but in Dallas, he is recorded as establishing the first brewery and producing the city's first locally made beer.

Monduel's beer was the only one to be found in Dallas for some time, but there is nothing to suggest his brewery existed past 1860, when he is listed as a cooper by trade in the United States Census. The *Dallas Herald* also implied no breweries were operating in late 1859, as it reveled in the news that a man named Wheeler was building one in the area. Wheeler's lager beer brewery was to be near Cedar Springs, and he promised to make a genuine article. It was the first local product in North Texas to be referred to as a "lager," which was fast becoming the country's best-selling type of beer after being introduced by Germans relocating to America in the 1840s. Wheeler's product was also the subject of what may have been the first advertisement for a North Texas brewery that November. In the piece, W.W. Peak and Brothers referred to themselves as the sole agents for Wheeler's Lager, which was available "in any quantity from one quart to forty gallons."

There was also talk that Wheeler was planning to operate a distillery alongside his brewery. The *Herald* was noticeably less enthusiastic on this point, considering it viewed lager beer as a "true temperance lecturer" able to reform "hard cases against their will." In showing an early bit of prohibitionist sentiment, the reporter even went on to express the opinion that Wheeler's beer would be "better and safer than mean, adulterated whiskey," if people would only drink it.

Like Monduel, Wheeler appears to have been in business for just a short time. From 1860 through the end of the Civil War, the only other reference to a brewer in Dallas is Roddolph Harpeeh. Likely a hobbyist, in 1860 the

Herald shows him being awarded a one-dollar premium for his lager beer at the Dallas County Agricultural Association's second annual fair. As for Monduel and Wheeler, there are no indications as to what became of their breweries, possibly closing due to economic conditions related to the coming war. Dallas endured a fire in July 1860 that destroyed most of the city's business district, but at least for Wheeler, his brewery was in another area of town altogether.

Regarding the Civil War, depending on where their businesses were located, brewers were affected in different ways from a production point of view. There was no rationing for the troops as there would be in later conflicts, but some Confederate states passed laws limiting grain usage in the manufacture of alcohol. In Union states, the industry's primary contribution to the war effort was to pay an excise tax that was passed as a part of the Internal Revenue Act of 1862 in an amount of one dollar per barrel of beer sold. As for Texas, by then the state had already seceded from the Union as of February 1, 1861, joining the Confederacy a month later.

When peace was restored, the barrel levy was just part of the postwar tax burden Texas brewers would bear once they rejoined the Union in 1870. Prior to the passage of the federal act, brewers in the state were assessed an occupation tax that became effective for the first time in January 1862. Essentially a license fee for doing business, it required a payment of twenty dollars from "each and every person or firm keeping any brewery." The amount would increase to as much as seventy-five dollars in January 1872 before returning to a prior level of fifty dollars in 1873. Combining this with eventual jumps in the federal rate would make it increasingly difficult for small brewers to compete against larger producers that were better able to absorb the additional costs.

One brewery whose timeline suggests taxation could have been an issue was the Dallas City Brewery. Located at Market and Wood Streets, it was built by August Mueller, a native of Switzerland who moved to Texas in 1868. Upon his arrival, Mueller went to work as a contractor and is credited with building many of the city's early structures. The business was run by Lewis and William Van Grinderbeck, brothers who were part of the Belgian contingent at La Reunion. Lewis (sometimes referred to as Louis) was the only one of the two identified as a brewer in the 1870 United States Census, but he may have had help from John Bassard, a German-born brewer who was living in the same precinct at the time. The brewery operated until February 1872, when a pair of ads appeared in the *Herald* seeking "a good, practical brewer, either to work for wages or rent the establishment with the whole apparatus." They were looking to fill the position immediately, or else the equipment would be sold for cash. No one appears to have taken them up on the offer.

For other brewers who opened after the war, taxes would continue to be a concern. Competition would eventually be another concern once John Neely Bryan realized his goal of bringing a rail connection to the city. He started a campaign to do so in 1866 after recognizing that the city's growth would be limited if not better able to trade with outside interests. When he finally succeeded in 1872, it would be a boon for Dallas economically. At the same time, it meant a more crowded marketplace was in the future for North Texas brewers.

UNLIKE DALLAS, Fort Worth remained unsettled prior to the Republic of Texas joining the United States in 1845. That act alone ignited a war with Mexico that went on until 1848, after which the government assigned Major General William Jenkins Worth to set up a line of defenses to protect settlements in the east from the untamed western frontier. Worth gave those under his command the task of selecting a North Texas defensive location, which was chosen to be at the junction of the West and Clear Forks of the Trinity River. The outpost would be established in 1849 and named in Worth's honor after his death in May of that year. It was officially designated as Fort Worth by the United States War Department.

The presence of the fort provided stability to the area, which encouraged settlement and the development of commerce. Besides farmers supplying fresh beef, there was a civilian general store and an established law practice within the first year of the soldiers' arrival. The progress led General Edward H. Tarrant to champion the formation of a county around the fort, leading to a bill creating Tarrant County in his name being signed into law in 1849. Though not originally voted as the county seat, Fort Worth would attain that title in later elections.

The military would eventually abandon the post in 1853, but a continuous flow of immigrants kept Fort Worth alive, and these new settlers began converting the old fort into a town. By the mid-1850s, businesses developed to the point where the people of Fort Worth had access to basic necessities. As for what there was to drink, more potent refreshment consisted of whiskey or cider early on, with the first saloon being traced to a package store opened by Noel Barton in the early 1850s. Another, called the First and Last Chance Saloon, followed in the 1860s, serving whiskey, peach brandy, gin and bitters. At that time, there was no mention of beer.

Indications are that the first brewery to appear in Fort Worth was built during the Civil War. Colonel Nathaniel Terry located it west of present-day Bennett Street facing the Trinity River. Terry was a former lieutenant governor of Alabama who moved to Fort Worth in 1854 after a failed gubernatorial bid. He was the town's most prominent slave owner at one time, with thirty-six slaves working a plantation he owned north of the fort. Slaves helped build the brewery as well, coming into being sometime after Terry sold the plantation and moved his family into town in July 1863. The purchaser of the property offered to make payment with $20,000 in gold, but being a secessionist, Terry would only accept the sum in Confederate currency. Some of this he converted to Confederate bonds, which were worthless after the Union's victory and left him financially ruined.

The war itself was hard on Fort Worth and Tarrant County. Population numbers in the county dropped from 6,000 to 1,000, with that of Fort Worth proper falling as low as 175. Homes were abandoned, and schools and businesses closed. It would be a few years before commerce started to pick up again, but by around 1868, the economy improved enough to see hints of expansion. Still, by the early 1870s, the population of Fort Worth only numbered about 300.

One of those who ended up in Fort Worth was Simon Mayer. He traveled from his native Germany in 1866 and, after a short stint in Milwaukee, settled in Texas around 1869. According to his obituary in a 1924 edition of the *Dallas Morning News*, Mayer established a brewery in Fort Worth before moving to Dallas in 1871. After the move, he continued in the business of alcohol in one form or another.

Other than Terry and Mayer, Fort Worth would not boast another brewery until 1891. By then, the town would be incorporated as a city, something that occurred in 1873, and the development of the Texas cattle industry would bring welcome prosperity to the area. The railroads would eventually reach Fort Worth as well, later being a factor in the decision of one man to build the largest pre-Prohibition brewery in North Texas.

OUTSIDE OF DALLAS AND FORT WORTH, only two other breweries appear to have existed in North Texas during the latter half of the 1800s. One was W.F. Both & Co. in Weatherford, of which little is known, and another was called the Cleburne Brewery when it got its start around 1868. It was founded by John Andrew Geupel, a "rugged frontiersman and adventuresome Texas pioneer." He fought in the Civil War during the Battle of Galveston in 1863 while serving with the Twentieth Texas Infantry in the Confederate army. After completing his service, he settled in Cleburne and built the brewery.

Geupel came to the United States from Wunsiedel, Germany, in 1848. His father started a brewery in Germany, which enabled Geupel to learn the trade while brewing the lagers of his homeland. While in Cleburne, he sold Old German Lager for $0.10 per bottle prior to taking on Fritz Wulfert as a partner and advertising "a superior article of lager beer" for $1.25 per dozen in May 1873. Perhaps the first North Texas brewer to sell beer in a twelve-pack, the new format was so popular that people no longer purchased Geupel's beer by the bottle.

Geupel made a success of the business for a while, but taxes eventually got the best of him. The federal excise tax had remained the same since inception, but Geupel was certainly subject to the state occupation tax increases of the early 1870s. After seven years, he entered into an agreement to sell the brewery to John and Elijah Guffee in April 1875. The brothers were issued a promissory note by Geupel, whereby they agreed to pay him "four hundred dollars with interest of two percent per annum" by November.

They operated the brewery over the next couple of years under the name Guffee Brothers and then Guffee and Guffee until such time that Elijah conveyed his full interest in the property to John in February 1878. Somewhere along the way, the Guffees became associated with a man named Mike Dixon. Elijah had taken to running a saloon, and Dixon was involved either as a partner or an employee. Although the three were said to be close friends, a conflict of some sort arose on the evening of November 29, 1878.

The disagreement started with news that Dixon had threatened John with a gun, and by the time it was over, both men were dead. At trial, witness testimony agreed on the basics of what occurred. John went to Dixon and waved a knife about his face and throat. Elijah, who had come to investigate with a rifle in hand, urged John to back off, but he ran up and seized Dixon again, who responded by firing a pistol and killing him. Within seconds, Elijah raised his rifle and gunned down Dixon in turn.

On the question of what caused events to escalate, the details of what transpired between Dixon and John Guffee were never fully determined. There was some discussion prior to the shooting about settling the dispute "by the books," leading to speculation that the men were at odds over money. In any event, one year later, a jury found Elijah guilty of murder in the first degree and sentenced him to life in prison. The Texas Court of Appeals reviewed the case in 1880 and overturned the verdict due to the jury not having been given instructions allowing them to consider Dixon's killing an act of justifiable homicide.

The case was to be retried that July in Johnson County, but the defendant requested a change in venue due to a perceived great prejudice against him. The request was granted, resulting in the hearing being moved to Somerville in Burleson County, and from there, the records turn cold. Some claim Elijah was sentenced to death and hanged, but his name does not appear in a listing of Texas executions dating back to 1819. Moreover, the only Elijah Guffee shown to have died in Cleburne did so in August 1878, over a year before the initial conviction, apparently the son of John Guffee born in 1870. It remains unclear what ultimately happened to Elijah; regardless, the Cleburne Brewery was no more.

2
TIMES OF TRANSITION
(1872–1881)

A crowd of five thousand people cheered the arrival of the first wood-burning locomotive as it steamed into Dallas in 1872. The train arrived on a newly built line of the Houston and Texas Central Railway (H&TC), and it marked a turning point for a city that had been previously isolated with no access to waterways for shipping. Less than a year later, the Texas and Pacific Railway (T&P) made a connection to the H&TC, and almost at once, a city of three thousand people in 1872 became an industrial center that was now home to over seven thousand.

There was a similar effect in Fort Worth once work was completed to route the T&P from Dallas in 1876. It was the first step in realizing what came to be known as the "Tarantula Map," a spider-like rendering of proposed rail lines going in and out of the city. Jesse Shenton Zane-Cetti, who would later play a key role in Fort Worth's brewing history, drew the map based on the vision of newspaper owner B.B. Paddock that was published in Paddock's *Fort Worth Democrat* in 1873. At the time, not a single railroad made a connection to Fort Worth. Paddock would play a role in making every line on the map a reality, each of which was constructed by 1885.

One connection made in 1873 was particularly significant. That year, the Missouri, Kansas and Texas Railroad (also referred to as the MKT and later the KT or the Katy) completed an extension to Denison, which had the effect of linking Dallas to St. Louis by way of the H&TC. Although roughly one hundred miles away, this line benefited Fort Worth's economy due to the city's growing presence in the cattle industry. Trail drives already going through Fort Worth had every reason to continue doing so on the way to Denison, where cars could be loaded with cattle for northern markets. As for area brewers, the Katy connected North Texas to one of the country's largest brewing centers. Despite ads for "bottled porter" in 1857 and others for "India Pale" ale and Christian Moerlein's Cincinnati Lager in 1870, most beer sold in and around Dallas and Fort Worth prior to the railroads was probably produced in Texas. Now local brewers would have to contend with the specter of increased competition from breweries outside the state.

Along with brewing strongholds in Cincinnati and Milwaukee, St. Louis formed a part of what came to be known as the "German Triangle." Being to the east, the natural progression of settlement in early America meant these cities were well established and brewing beer before Dallas was founded. More importantly, they each benefited from a wave of German settlers in the 1840s and 1850s, who brought with them the rich brewing heritage of the Old World. A portion of that wave washed over Texas as well, but those who came with it chose to settle to the south in the Hill Country around Austin, and it is there that many of the state's earliest breweries were built.

After 1872, St. Louis brewers William J. Lemp and E. Anheuser & Co. (the predecessor to Anheuser-Busch) joined Moerlein of Cincinnati in being among the first national brands to be sold in North Texas. Large-scale brewing would not occur in Dallas for another decade, and it would take even longer for the same to happen in Fort Worth. Soon, the products of Frank Falk and Joseph Schlitz of Milwaukee were also available locally, meaning all three corners of the German Triangle were represented in the regional market before brewing in North Texas could be considered an industrial enterprise.

Given this environment, it could not have been easy for a home-based brewer like Charles Meisterhans, but he recognized who he was up against and challenged them head-on. Ads in April 1873 touted the availability of his "FRESH BEER" in bold capital letters, saying it was "equal in body and flavor to the best St. Louis or Cincinnati beer." Most likely, he was targeting Moerlein's product, as well as Lemp's "celebrated St. Louis Lager." Both were selling in Dallas around the time the brewery at his 804 Bryan Street residence was in operation.

Meisterhans's wife, Francisca, actually started the business. She was married previously to a man named Jetzer, and after the Civil War, the couple traveled with their young daughter from Marshall, Texas, to open a brewery in Dallas. Brewing was not new to them, as tax records show they had been in the business at their former home throughout 1866. Unfortunately, during the trip her husband became ill and was put to bed in a wagon. While tossing and turning in response to a fever, he somehow shot himself with his own pistol.

Thereafter, the party came upon a house owned by Henry and Elizabeth Boll, a couple with a reputation for taking in weary travelers. The Bolls tried to tend to Jetzer's wounds, but he passed away. They opened their home to the widow and her daughter, who stayed with them in the years prior to Francisca's marriage to Meisterhans. In the interim, Francisca went on with the plans for a brewery. In September 1869, she took out an ad in the *Dallas Weekly Herald* declaring her "brewery in full operation" where you could enjoy "the best of lager beer…at five cents per glass."

Her benefactors were the reason Francisca came to know Charles Meisterhans. He was the nephew of Henry Boll, himself a La Reunion colonist who was among the first Swiss settlers in 1855. Meisterhans was twenty-four years old in 1870 when he made his way from Switzerland to America, where Boll gave him work to help him adjust to his new life. He married Francisca in 1871 and would soon take over the operation of the brewery, which he ran until at least early 1875. That year, Meisterhans is last referenced as a brewer in the Dallas City Directory. The occupation tax, and how it disadvantaged small brewers, was cited as his reason for abandoning the enterprise.

Besides Meisterhans, three other brewers appear in the 1875 Dallas City Directory. One was William Jogel (or Jegel in the 1878 guide), who lived in a tenant house at 1016 Main Street, but it is not known if he operated a home brewery or worked with others who are listed that year. Easier to associate with a known location are brewers named C. Euste and S. Meyer. These men were living at 812 Bryan Street, an address that would eventually be home to E. Arnoldi & Co. in 1878. Sources differ about who owned the property leading up to that point.

Both the *Register of United States Breweries, 1876–1976* and *American Breweries II* refer to the brewery at 812 Bryan Street as Klein & Wolff beginning in 1875. However, Samuel Klein and Simon Wolff (or Wolf) were partners in a wholesale liquor firm by the same name, which they moved to Galveston prior to July 1875, and references to that effect do not mention the two being involved in a brewery. Whether they were or not, by 1878 Ernest Arnoldi and Gustav H. Schmidt took over as proprietors and ran E. Arnoldi & Co. for about a year before the company's namesake moved to Sherman and became one of its most regarded citizens. A native of Germany, Arnoldi was the city's agent for Anheuser-Busch prior to negotiating the purchase of that company's ice plant and organizing the Sherman Ice Company. He was both president and manager of the business until his death in September 1915.

CHARLES MEISTERHANS AND SIMON MAYER both moved on after early forays as brewers and found success in other areas of the industry. The idea of brewing again was seemingly never far from either man's mind, but they each made a mark on Dallas as proprietors of one of the city's early *biergartens*. It was a lack of recreational facilities in Dallas that led to the development of biergartens during the 1870s. The city acquired the land for its first park in 1876, but the caretaker's duties involved nothing more than tending the grounds and closing the gates promptly at 6:00 p.m.

"Meager" was how one newspaper described the park, as for years, not much was offered in the way of relaxation or enjoyment. Biergartens proved a more attractive alternative. Such establishments were a few steps up from the average saloon, and though the name might suggest otherwise, there was more to do than just drink beer. These were family-friendly destinations with varied activities, often referred to as pleasure resorts or amusement parks.

One of the earliest biergartens was developed by Ben Long, yet another La Reunion colonist who came to Dallas in 1855. He built Long's Lake in 1874 on a thirty-six-acre tract of land with an artificial lake near the Trinity River (in the vicinity of present-day Stemmons at Oak Lawn). Rides on the water were a main attraction, and it is said he had boats named for each of his five children. He knew Charles Meisterhans from back home, having brought the would-be Dallas brewer to America during a return trip from Switzerland in 1870.

Meisterhans started his venture around 1873 in association with his brewery. Located on Bryan Street near Hall, when Meisterhans's garden was first established, it took up a third of a city block. "The only quiet and comfortable place in the city for the resort of families" had tenpin alleys, target shooting and a pavilion that served as a bandstand. It was a gathering place for German and Swiss settlers living in the surrounding area, and Sunday concerts were a regular occurrence. There was no charge to get in, and Meisterhans invited work-weary patrons to come by and enjoy fresh beer while listening to "as fine a music as can be heard in any quarter of the world."

As fate would have it, Meisterhans ended up running Long's Lake for a time after its founder was shot and killed while intervening in a bar dispute. An October 1877 announcement in the *Dallas Daily Herald* shows Meisterhans as proprietor of Long's business, roughly a month before he turned over day-to-day operation of his own biergarten to Simon Mayer. Meisterhans would eventually become the local representative for William J. Lemp in 1881, but not before partnering with Mayer in the Apollo Hall, a separate venture described as the "largest and most elegant beer hall in Texas." The saloon offered a variety of whiskeys, fine wines and cigars, but Lemp's was the exclusive beer. This was probably not a coincidence because Mayer actually predated Meisterhans as the city's agent for the St. Louis brewer. Mayer would go on to do other things as well once he left the Apollo and Meisterhans's garden to open his own business. It would be called Mayer's Garden, and it would become the most celebrated biergarten in the city's history.

Mayer's Garden occupied not one but two physical addresses on Elm Street in Dallas when it debuted in 1881. The main building consisted of a three-story structure with a basement that was used to contain the kitchen. A restaurant and saloon took up the first floor, with rooms for rent and a music hall on the remaining two levels. On the outside were landscaped grounds that stretched across the block to Pacific Avenue, "filled with trees, vines, arbors and fountains laid off beautifully with graveled walks" in a setting reminiscent of a rustic retreat. Performances of all types occurred nightly on a provided stage, and it is said that some of the top attractions of the day appeared there. Mayer also had a collection of exotic animals that served as the city's first zoo, operating before the Dallas City Zoo was established in 1888. It was an impressive array of entertainment for what was considered to be a bold enterprise at the time, especially since admission was free.

For years, Mayer's Garden was the place to see and be seen in Dallas. As a testament to its prominence, it was the first business in the city to get outdoor electric lights after workers completed the wiring in August 1882. They were arc lights, and onlookers said they made the older gas lamps appear pale by comparison. Mayer installed six of them in all, placing lights at the entrance, inside the music hall and over the fountain in the middle of the park.

As for what brought it to an end, Mayer's only son, William, told the *Dallas Morning News* in 1933 that his father gave up on the business after the advent of the more restrictive Sunday-closing laws in the 1890s. These laws were enacted to either regulate or prohibit the opening of certain businesses

Mayer's Garden offered patrons a variety of entertainment options and was the place to see and be seen in early Dallas, circa 1885. *From the collections of the Texas/Dallas History and Archives Division, Dallas Public Library.*

on Sunday to encourage people to attend church. For Mayer, Sunday was his busiest time when people would spend the day enjoying food and drink ahead of the workweek. Lunch plates and beer were the only items that came with a cost at the Garden, and the loss of revenue was more than his father could overcome. By 1902, Mayer had closed up shop and moved out of the city.

In addition to their biergartens, both Mayer and Meisterhans explored a return to brewing later in their careers even though their earlier efforts had stalled. Mayer opened his Berliner Weiss Beer Brewery at the same location as his biergarten around 1894, operating it until a fire in 1899. He tried once more, apparently partnering with a local liquor wholesaler to open Mayer & Bruce. It lasted less than four months—assuming it ever went into production at all—and closed before the end of 1901.

Meisterhans, who spent over thirty years as the Dallas agent for William J. Lemp, planned a new brewery in June 1905. He and partner Adolph

Feickert purchased Lemp's facility on Crowdus Street after the owner and company patriarch committed suicide. Investors were brought together, and a charter was filed for the Columbia Manufacturing Company. The newly acquired ice and cold storage plant was to have brewing equipment installed, but that never came to pass. It remained solely an ice-manufacturing concern until the site was leased to a Tennessee-based dairy company around 1920.

3
BREWING ON AN INDUSTRIAL SCALE (1884–1893)

In the fall of 1881, the *Dallas Herald* suggested that if a lager beer brewery were built in the city, there was a substantial profit to be made. It had been two years since the closing of E. Arnoldi & Co. left Dallas without a brewery. At the same time, with no other active breweries in North Texas, a lack of local flavor was a common theme across the region.

Up to this point, breweries in Texas had been small in scope. Many were based in individual homes and generated minimal volume. Tax records show Francisca Jetzer's operation in Marshall, prior to her move to Dallas and marriage to Charles Meisterhans, resulted in average sales of just over a dozen barrels per month in 1866. Even smaller was W.F. Both & Co. in Weatherford, a brewery that sold a total of forty-nine barrels during 1878. The occupation tax increases of the early 1870s were certainly a factor in the dwindling number of small breweries, but for those that carried on, such limited production offered little hope for competing with the likes of the Anheuser-Busch Brewing Association and William J. Lemp. Local or not, the changing business climate was shifting to favor those who were able to brew on a larger scale.

The first to up the ante in Dallas was Anton Wagenhauser. Born in Bayern, Germany, Wagenhauser moved to the city shortly after selling his interest in a St. Louis malt house in February 1884. By December, he broke ground and laid the cornerstone for a company he would charter as the Wagenhauser Brewing Association. A total of $100,000 was invested in the firm, $60,000 of which was put up by Wagenhauser himself.

Construction took four months, allowing brewing operations to commence in April and a charter to be filed in May 1885. Reputed to be one of the largest in the southern United States, the steam-powered brewery was outfitted with the most modern equipment and capable of producing up to two hundred barrels per day. Typical of large breweries, the company also manufactured ice in addition to beer. It was a natural extension of the business as lagers were produced and refrigeration was necessary to maintain proper fermentation temperatures for those types of beers.

A June 13 grand opening featured a lavish parade and banquet drawing local dignitaries and fellow business owners. Area newspapers covered the event, publishing viewpoints from both sides of the growing prohibitionist debate. By this time, brewers across the country were contending daily with those seeking to put an end to the industry as a whole. Conservative forces were persisting in their push to instill reform, telling all who would listen about the evils of alcohol and how it had led to the moral decline of American society. The opening of a brewery provided the ideal platform for the opposing sides to let their opinions be known.

Before the festivities were even announced, an article in the *Dallas Weekly Herald* took up the anti argument and outlined how the brewery would benefit the local economy. It pointed to things like the creation of new jobs, increased tax revenues for the city and the greater profit potential for regional grain suppliers. These benefits, the author noted, should have been "evident to every clear-headed and impartial man," and they would be lost if the city were to succumb to the "iron and aggressive rule of prohibitionists."

Those arguing the other side found their voice in letters to the editor of the daily and weekly editions of the *Fort Worth Gazette*. One letter that was dated the day of the brewery's opening portrayed the coming event as an anti-temperance demonstration more likely put on by local liquor sellers. Proclaiming beer to be responsible for the desecration of the Sabbath, it called for Dallas mayor John Henry Brown to forego a reportedly scheduled appearance in light of the belief that his election was due to the vote of temperance men. Whether or not that was the reason, the mayor did not attend. The *Gazette* attributed the no-show to sickness while painting the affair in a positive light, going on to call it a grand celebration with not a single drunken man to be found.

A separate letter expressed outrage over the "drunken orgie," further accusing the Fort Worth and Dallas newspapers of showing favor to the liquor interests. It went on to call out the *Gazette* for falsely reporting on the mayor's absence. Rather than sickness, it was contended, the mayor had given an interview saying he never promised to attend. As for the celebration, one writer called the turnout laughable and no more worthy of attention than a circus procession.

Whatever the truth, Dallas now had a brewery poised to do battle with the national brands on the city's home turf. Like others would do both before and after him, Wagenhauser hoped to defend his ground by placing emphasis on the idea that fresh, local beer was better. A separate article published on the brewery's big day listed reasons why his product fit such a description. Wagenhauser's "home-made beer" was declared superior to the "imported medicated beer" made available from out-of-state producers. "Drugs" referred to additives brewers used to preserve beer during long transport, something his product did not contain. It was also free of adjuncts like corn and glucose, which was the basis for billing it as "absolutely pure," a selling point touted along with the local theme the following week in the *Herald*: "Wagenhauser beer is pure and whenever you spend five cents on this beer you get value received, and your money stays at home. Patronize your home brewery."

The temperance movement directly influenced another tactic breweries would use over time to sell their beer. Proclamations that beer was bad for the mind, body and soul were countered with statements like: "All who have tried the Wagenhauser beer say it is decidedly the best and purest beer ever in the market. It will restore to you your health and add vigor and strength to your broken constitution. Let everybody who wants to enjoy good health during this hot summer drink Wagenhauser beer."

Despite the promotional bluster, any success Wagenhauser had was short-lived. September brought a rumor that he planned to move the brewery to Fort Worth, presumably due to a lack of local support in Dallas. By April 1886, he was being sued for $780 by Paul Glucksman, an investor and officer in the brewery who served as second vice-president. Glucksman prevailed, but the sheriff had to levy a set of wagons to pay off the judgment. Wagenhauser was also behind on water payments, the collection of which was referred to the city attorney. It all came to a head in April, when the brewery was sold to satisfy creditors.

Wagenhauser would go on to run a bottling business in the city, packaging Tony Faust beer for Anheuser-Busch in the late 1880s. He even explored the idea of building another brewery in Fort Worth just two years after the loss of his original venture. That did not happen, but he did open the Dallas Weiss Beer Brewery sometime around 1891. The first brewery of its kind in North Texas, it employed five men and was located at 221 College Avenue, the same address as his bottle works. He ran both operations until his death in 1898.

The Wagenhauser brewery went up for auction after Frederick Wolf of Chicago foreclosed on a trust deed issued to him by the Wagenhauser Brewing Association. An ice machine manufacturer, Wolf supplied the brewery with equipment and accessories valued at $35,000, which combined with incidental expenses, brought the total due him to $50,000. When the note securing this amount went unpaid, the brewery was put up for sale to collect payment. At auction, Wolf placed a bid equal to his claim and won out over Dallas contractor P.J. Butler, who offered $10,000. A deed was issued to Wolf on the property at the corner of Houston and Cochran Streets (now McKinney Avenue), but Butler had a separate claim on the brewery that would become central to a long-running legal drama.

Wolf transferred ownership to James J. and John J. Gannon in June 1886 by way of a warranty deed, maintaining a lien on the property in the amount of $32,000. This agreement contained a covenant against encumbrances, making Wolf responsible for any liens that might be established on the brewery. Once the transaction closed, the Gannon brothers set about making improvements to bring the value of the brewery up to $150,000. Eventually, they formed a joint-stock corporation with Michael Keeley and R.C. Gannon of Chicago. Although Keeley was the head of the Keeley Brewing Company of Chicago, the Gannons were residents of Dallas and would run the brewery as a strictly local enterprise. It was chartered as the Dallas Brewing Company in October 1886.

Meanwhile, Butler filed suit against Wagenhauser in May 1885 over unpaid amounts related to construction work done during the brewery's development, asserting what was referred to as a mechanic's lien. Seeking to protect his interests and prevent foreclosure, Wolf retained counsel and made it known he wished to be involved in the proceedings. However, unknown to Wolf and his attorneys, the case was called to hearing near the end of November 1886, despite never being scheduled on the court calendar. A verdict was handed down in favor of Butler with the judge ordering the sale of the brewery to recover on his claim of $6,088.80. According to the minutes of the court, the result was a settlement consented to by Butler and Wagenhauser. Nowhere was it mentioned that Wolf had an interest in the case or that the Gannons had legally purchased the brewery in June. Nevertheless, the property was sold at auction to W.L. Griggs in January 1887 for $8,000.

Such was the state of affairs two days later when the *Dallas Morning News* published an article summarizing the case, appropriately titled "The Dallas Brewery Muddle." Wolf obtained an injunction blocking the January sale, but the court denied his request to verify the legitimacy and amount of Butler's claim. He filed the first in a series of appeals, resulting in the "celebrated brewery suit" remaining in dispute until at least 1894 after rulings by both the Texas Supreme Court and the Court of Civil Appeals. Wolf would seemingly never invalidate the lien, but the improper sale to Griggs remained permanently vacated.

As for the rightful owners of the brewery, the Gannons had issues of their own. The Northwestern National Bank acquired the note Wolf issued to the brothers in 1886. With unpaid principal and interest totaling $15,724 as of August 1889, the bank moved to foreclose. The brothers tried to argue that the existence and pending nature of the Butler lien affected the value of the property and, by extension, the amount being called due. This case was also heard by the Texas Supreme Court, which disagreed in saying the Gannons had established a negotiable contract with Wolf, which by definition, was payable without condition.

The brewery continued to operate, although it is unclear if the past due amount was paid or if the bank assumed control. James J. Gannon was still involved as of April 1890, but he departed shortly thereafter. His brother John is listed as manager in the 1891 city directory, whereas a *Dallas Morning News* story indicates Alderman Samuel Klein acquired an interest and served as president until he sold his shares in March 1891. Later that same year, workers went on strike in June seeking higher wages, an occurrence immediately followed by the brewery going into receivership. James J. Gannon, by now engaged in the development of a brewery in Fort Worth, returned briefly to oversee operations prior to the appointment of W.J. Betterton as receiver to handle the eventual sale.

When Thomas F. Keeley, now president of the Keeley Brewing Company of Chicago after the death of his father, Michael, made the commitment to purchase the brewery outright in February 1893, it was the third time the property had changed hands in only eight years of existence. At this point, it was a brewery perhaps more famous for its courtroom appearances than for its beer. What Keeley acquired for his bid of $50,000 was a five-acre facility with a four-story main building and attached bottling house adjacent to the Missouri, Kansas and Texas rail yard.

The Gannons placed revenue estimates in the range of $200,000 in late 1886, but that was based on production numbers of only a couple hundred barrels per month. Changes made since then had bumped output to around fifteen thousand barrels per year by July 1891. Still, when Keeley chartered the Dallas Brewery in April 1893, he pledged further updates to make it better able to compete in the marketplace. It was a wise move, considering the playing field in North Texas had recently become more crowded.

JAMES J. GANNON HAD NO INTENTION of getting back into the brewing business after leaving the Dallas Brewing Company in the spring of 1890. His plan was to spend time traveling, which he did while visiting Mexico and cities across Texas. A stopover in Fort Worth is what changed his mind. A friend took him to see an artesian well that was recently built in the city. Gannon took note of how the well's output was cleaner than the muddy Dallas water he was used to, and he wondered if it might make good beer. He collected samples and sent them to a chemist, who confirmed that Fort Worth water was well suited for brewing. Along with the city's favorable access to the railways, the water quality encouraged Gannon to build what would become Fort Worth's largest industrial enterprise.

Bids were taken, and a contract was awarded for building the Texas Brewing Company in September 1890. Work began on the seven-story brewhouse and supporting structures later that month at the corner of Jones and Ninth Streets. Operations got underway the following March with seventy-five workers on the payroll and a startup system designed to brew 250-barrel batches. A charter was filed indicating a capital stock authorization of $150,000 with principal officers to be Gannon as president, Jesse Shenton Zane-Cetti as vice-president and secretary and J.C. McCarthy as treasurer.

Almost as soon as the initial construction was complete, the brewery looked to expand by securing an adjacent block and announcing additional work before the first beer hit the market in May 1891. It was an ambitious venture with fully a half million dollars invested in the firm by June and with annual revenue projected to be close to $1 million. Within a year, the brewery employed 160 workers and, through additional improvements, had boosted production capacity to 250,000 barrels per year. The brewery also manufactured one hundred tons of ice daily. It was declared to be the largest brewery and ice plant in the South.

Production numbers suggested it was making enough beer to distribute outside of Texas, and the brewery did eventually send shipments to neighboring states Oklahoma and New Mexico. However, from the beginning, Gannon recognized the importance of winning over local consumers. Shortly after the brewery opened, he gave an interview where

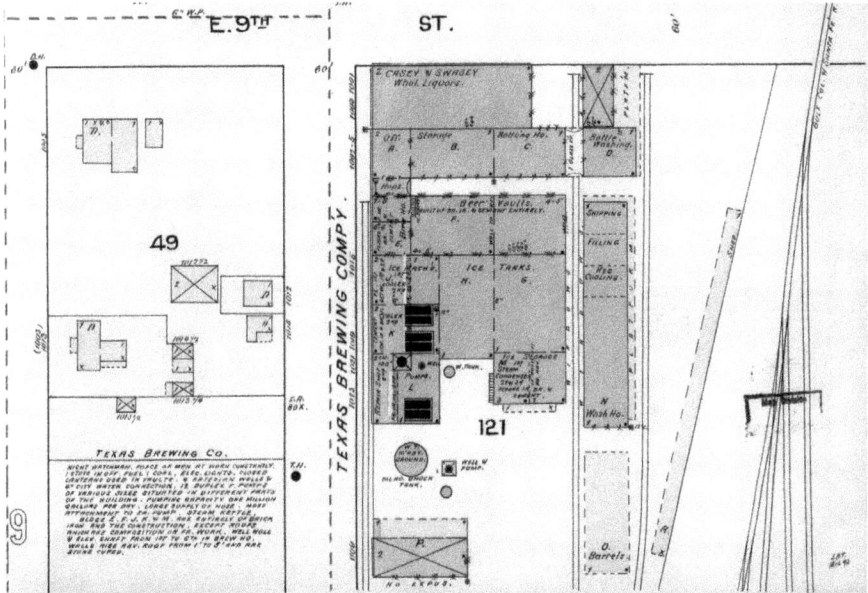

The Texas Brewing Company took up the better part of a city block in 1893, as shown in a Sanborn Fire Insurance Map from that year. *From the University of Texas Libraries.*

Bottling at the Texas Brewing Company, circa 1895. *From the collections of the Texas/Dallas History and Archives Division, Dallas Public Library.*

Jesse Shenton Zane-Cetti served as president of the Texas Brewing Company from 1895 until Prohibition. *Courtesy of the Freemasons of Fort Worth Lodge No.148.*

he said that people "think anything made at home cannot be as good as that made in another state, so we have made a better beer than they could buy anywhere else." Before long, the phrase "Patronize Home Industry" was to be found on virtually all brewery signage and advertisements. The brewery did its part as well, sourcing materials needed for day-to-day operations from businesses located within Fort Worth whenever possible.

Gannon would go on to say that the "appreciation of the people of Texas for good beer" was what fueled expansion, something that was a recurring theme throughout the brewery's first decade. Martin Casey, a principal stockholder and owner of a wholesale liquor business adjacent to the brewery, commented after taking over as president in 1893 that "we are nearly always making improvements." Same-year growth numbers on the order of 80 percent show why that was the case. Casey implied the number would be even higher if the current facility had more space for cellar and refrigeration capacity.

Two years later, Casey was succeeded as president by Zane-Cetti, who, prior to helping found the brewery, had already played a major role in the development of Fort Worth. Besides being responsible for drawing the "Tarantula Map," he helped organize the Tarrant County Construction Company for the purposes of completing a leg of the Texas & Pacific railroad between Dallas and Fort Worth. Later, he was involved in fundraising efforts to bring the Santa Fe Railway to the city, an offshoot of which would run next to the brewery as part of the Gulf, Colorado and Santa Fe Railroad. In recognition of his contributions to the city, a historical marker bearing his name once existed at 901 Commerce Street associated with a structure he built there in 1889. Despite the significance, the building was demolished in 1970.

4
ANTI-TRUST AND ADOLPHUS BUSCH (1892–1909)

Small-scale outfits still popped up occasionally, but those that opened around the turn of the century lasted no more than a year or two. These included Mayer & Bruce and the Excelsior Weiss Beer Brewery (1901) in Dallas, along with the Mingus Brewing Company (1908–1909) in Palo Pinto County west of Fort Worth. Another brewery slated for Dallas, the work of a local liquor seller named C.H. Huvelle, declared its intent to begin operations in October 1900 but was listed as closed in January 1901, seemingly never having gone into production.

Fort Worth's brewery and its Dallas counterpart were the only two active operations in North Texas at the beginning of 1900. The Texas Brewing Company was the larger of the two, able to produce 250,000 barrels a year compared to only 75,000 for the Dallas Brewery. The Dallas Brewery's first order of business in 1900 was to spend upward of $75,000 on additions. The plans included a bottling house, storage house, wash house, office building and stable. It took on an even grander project in 1907, investing $180,000 to build a seven-story building that would contain a new brewhouse, stock mill and ice factory.

In Fort Worth, the Texas Brewing Company approached its second decade much the same way as it had the first. Perpetual change had grown the plant from the confines of a city block to a sprawling four-and-three-quarters-acre complex. In 1901, it took up "the entire block from 9th to 12th Street and from Jones to the main track of the Santa Fe railroad." Soon, a new bottling plant was in the works to be followed by two additional ice storage

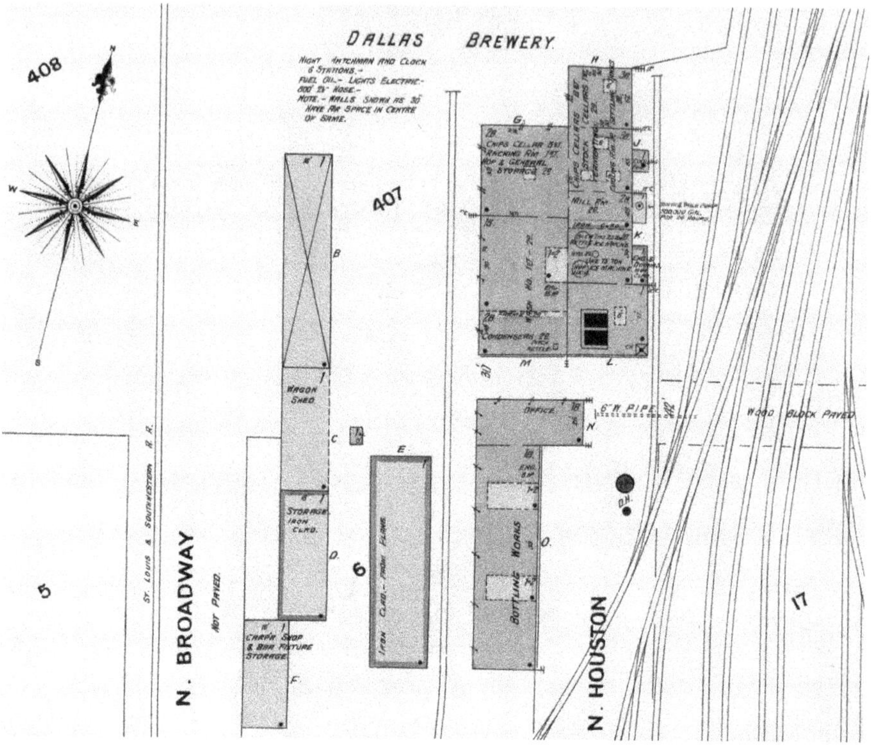
DALLAS BREWERY
NIGHT WATCHMAN AND CLOCK 6 STATIONS.-
FUEL OIL.- LIGHTS ELECTRIC.-
NOTE.- WALLS SHOWN AS 30" HAVE AIR SPACE IN CENTRE OF SAME.
408
407
WAGON SHED
STORAGE IRON CLAD
CARP'R SHOP & BAR FIXTURE STORAGE
OFFICE
BOTTLING WORKS
6" W. PIPE
WOOD BLOCK PAVED
5
6
17
ST. LOUIS & SOUTHWESTERN R.R.
N. BROADWAY
NOT PAVED
N. HOUSTON

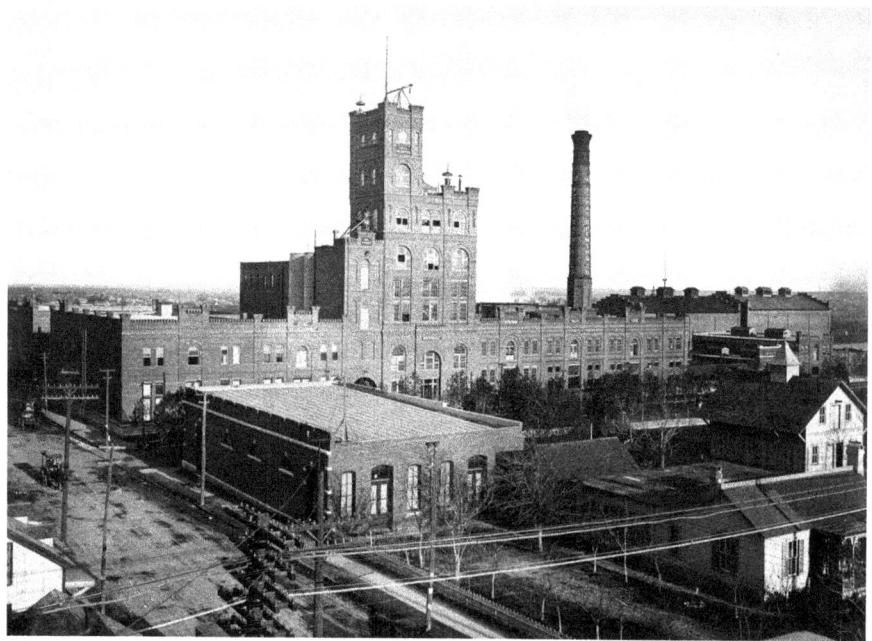

buildings, which were in place by 1903. That year, the combined revenue of the business was estimated to be in the range of $1.5 million.

How the two breweries marketed their products was changing as well. Instead of continuing to offer a generic-sounding "pure lager beer," the Dallas Brewery developed brands like Home Beer, Tipperary Beer and eventually White Rose Beer. Promotional language for each followed the anti-prohibition custom of promoting health in some form or fashion, with White Rose ads saying it had the "stamp of approval of physicians and scientific men." The beer was even formulated to be "especially mild for family use." As for Tipperary, listings suggested it was "splendid nourishment," made "absolutely pure and free from germ contamination, having undergone the process of boiling."

The Texas Brewing Company followed a similar approach by advertising products promising to tend to your physical and mental well-being: "There's nothing better…against indigestion, insomnia and all other nervous troubles than the Texas Brewing Co.'s…Crown Bottle Beer!" Other ads suggested its beers might make you more attractive: "Household Beer…not only quenches the thirst but it puts color in the cheek, brightens the eye and revitalizes the blood; all of which means health and physical charm."

Household Beer and Crown Beer were among many brand names the Fort Worth brewery sold over time. It also had a seasonal Bock Beer it placed on the market in March 1895. Its most celebrated beer came in 1904 as a result of winning a gold medal at the Louisiana Purchase Exhibition, an event sometimes referred to as the St. Louis World's Fair. During the years that followed, Gold Medal Beer was featured in bold letters on the cover of the Fort Worth city directory. The accompanying tagline said, "When you buy Gold Medal Beer at the price of common beer, you are getting double value."

A 1904 listing in the *Dallas Morning News* showed a dozen quart bottles of "Dallas beer" priced at $1.65 compared to $2.25 for products from William J. Lemp, Anheuser-Busch and the Houston-based American Brewing Company. Pints were available if you preferred a smaller size, priced at

---

Opposite, top: The layout of the Dallas Brewing Company as it appeared in a 1905 Sanborn Fire Insurance Map. *From the University of Texas Libraries.*

Opposite, bottom: A view of the Texas Brewing Company in Fort Worth, circa 1900. *Courtesy of W.D. Smith Commercial Photography Collection, Special Collections, the University of Texas at Arlington Library, Arlington, Texas.*

$1.05 compared to $1.25 for the other brands (also for sale were 12.7-ounce split bottles). Around that same time, a dozen pints of "Fort Worth beer" could be had for $1.25, whereas quarts would run you $2.00. That made these products more expensive than beer brewed in Dallas and closer in price to out-of-state products like Budweiser, Schlitz and Pabst.

From an operational perspective, the new century brought stability for the Dallas brewery and business as usual for its counterpart in Fort Worth. The leadership of both companies remained in place during the years that followed, and each seemed to be on a path of growth and expansion. However, there would be bumps in the road, and the first would come in 1901.

Texas attorney general Charles K. Bell filed suit accusing ten breweries that were doing business in the state of violating anti-trust law by conspiring to fix the price of beer. One of the terms of an agreement entered into by breweries in February 1899 spoke to that effect: "Beer shall be valued at average cost price, not less than $2.50 per barrel." Fines would be set at anywhere from $200 to $5,000 per day, and each day was considered a separate offense. Some defendants were being tried on violations dating back well over a year, meaning they might be liable for millions of dollars in penalties. The state was seeking $3,209,500 from the Dallas Brewery alone.

A compromise was quickly drawn up whereby the breweries pled guilty in exchange for paying a reduced fine. They also forfeited their charters, but this was just a matter of resubmitting the necessary paperwork to get up and running again. One case observer commented to the *Fort Worth Register* that the move by the breweries to settle was indicative of the strength of the anti-trust laws. It was a fair point, especially as the law had been upheld against early challenges. For the breweries, it was more about self-preservation. A lawyer for the Texas Brewing Company explained his client's position in this way: "To defend against this law and be convicted would mean utter destruction of any ordinary corporation or individual, hence when the state brings a suit, a defendant must settle or risk probable annihilation. We contend that we are not guilty of violating the law, but prudence dictated that we make a compromise, rather than incur such risks."

Seven breweries based in Texas ended up paying $7,500 each, with three out-of-state breweries assessed individual fines of $15,000. All together, the state collected $97,500 in penalties. Afterward, there was talk of the Texas breweries consolidating and being managed by a single corporation, but in the end, they filed for new charters individually and went on about their business.

A Full-Bodied History of Brewing in Dallas, Fort Worth and Beyond

William J. Lemp and Adolphus Busch were among those forced to pay fines related to the anti-trust settlement of 1901. Both men had been doing business in North Texas since the mid-1870s, and each held a controlling interest in the Texas Brewing Company of Fort Worth after a management shakeup in April 1895. However, neither would ever build a brewery in the region. Lemp, who had perhaps the largest ice and cold storage facility in Dallas among out-of-state producers in the pre-Prohibition era, discussed but did not follow through on plans to add brewing equipment to his factory. Originally built in 1895 on Crowdus Street, it was the same plant Meisterhans and Feickert would purchase with similar intent ten years later.

As for Busch, he first visited Dallas in 1878 and during that trip left with the impression that "there were not more than a dozen respectable houses in the place." Upon his return in 1889, he was so taken with the amount of growth he witnessed that he declared it to be the "banner city of Texas." He had purchased an interest in the Lone Star Brewing Company of San Antonio a few years prior, and he was looking to make additional investments in the state. Building a brewery in Dallas was a possibility, but he had concerns about the water. He felt the city's artesian wells needed to be dug to three times their current depth. Deeper wells, he believed, yielded purer water at higher pressure. The greater force was something many brewers using well water looked for in that it provided a better flow rate. Improve upon these factors, Busch implied, and he would be more likely to consider locating a brewery in Dallas.

At least from a brewing perspective, Busch's attitude changed dramatically over the next three years. The condition of the water seemed to become the furthest thing from his mind; as of 1892, the issue was climate. During an interview that year, a reporter asked if beer could be brewed successfully in the South. To this, Busch replied, "A kind of beer can be made here, but not good beer." He explained the reason had to do with the yeast, claiming that artificially cooling it caused spoilage and that the region's extreme temperature variations were equally detrimental to its health. Either, he said, resulted in undesirable changes to the character of the beer. Based on this factor, he was of the opinion that "all of the breweries in the south have proved more or less a failure."

The reporter followed up by asking if he would ever consider brewing in this part of the country, to which Busch responded, "I would never think of making fine beer in this country." In addition to Lone Star Brewing, by this time, Busch was involved in the development of the Galveston Brewing

Dallas headquarters of the William J. Lemp Brewing Company of St. Louis, Missouri, circa 1895. *From the collections of the Texas/Dallas History and Archives Division, Dallas Public Library.*

Company southeast of Houston. Knowing this, Zane-Cetti of the Texas Brewing Company pointed out the obvious disconnect: "He says he would never think of making fine beer in this country, yet he owns one brewery, the Lone Star in San Antonio, and is building another in Houston."

Herman Zimmerman, brewer for the Dallas Brewing Company, questioned Busch's statements as well. Leading a reporter into the brewery's cold room, he asked, "What is the difference whether this temperature is produced by the North Pole or by brine running through pipes? The effect is the same on the article cooled." He also noted that the brewery's refrigeration system varied only a few degrees between summer and winter. Following a similar train of thought, Zane-Cetti delivered the retort, "For me to answer Mr. Busch's remarks from a scientific standpoint would render him most ridiculous." The whole charade led the *Fort Worth Daily Gazette* to conclude that Busch was well on his way to convincing "the public that he sometimes talks out of his hat."

Looking at the interview from a practical point of view, Texas Brewing Company president James J. Gannon believed it was all just a ploy. He thought Busch might be trying to discourage further investment in Texas from outside interests. In that way, Busch would have the upper hand should he choose to add to his business in the state—or he was trying to devalue

After it was completed in 1912, the Adolphus Hotel was, for a time, the tallest building in Texas. *From the collections of the Texas/Dallas History and Archives Division, Dallas Public Library.*

A vintage postcard depicting the Busch Building in downtown Dallas, circa 1914. *From the collection of Brian Brown.*

Texas-made beer such that he might gain a greater share in the marketplace. This latter assumption may have been closer to the truth based on Busch's acquisition of the Alamo Brewing Company of San Antonio in 1895. It was believed that the move was made solely to eliminate intracity competition with his Lone Star Brewing Company.

By 1895, the company line was that the brewery in St. Louis was well equipped to supply North Texas. Although he would never have his name on a brewery in Dallas, Adolphus Busch managed to leave his mark on the city in other ways. He remarked once that "a good hotel would always do more to attract a city than almost any other inducement." In Dallas, he built two: one was the Oriental Hotel, which occupied the corner of Commerce and Akard Streets from 1893 until it was demolished to make room for another development in 1924. The other is the Adolphus Hotel at 1321 Commerce Street. Completed in 1912, the twenty-two-story complex was once the tallest building in Texas.

He also bankrolled the Busch Building at 1509 Main Street. It opened in 1913 before eventually being sold to a Houston businessman and renamed the Kirby Building. Today, it houses residential apartments and is known as the Kirby Residences on Main. Along with the Adolphus Hotel, it is listed in the National Register of Historic Places. Unfortunately, failing health prevented Busch from seeing either prior to his death in October 1913.

5
TEXAS TEMPERANCE AND LOCAL OPTION (1837–1882)

To be wet or to be dry—that was the question, and it was one that Texans were asking as far back as the 1840s. It started years before Dallas and Fort Worth were incorporated as cities, with those who settled what would become the Republic of Texas bringing temperance sentiment with them from other parts of the country.

In both a literal and figurative sense, Prohibition would be the end-all roughly eighty years later, but for early reformers, it was not about total abstinence. It was about not drinking more than was good for you, and sometimes, beer did not even factor into the equation. In the late 1700s and early 1800s, reforms in other states singled out distilled liquors rather than milder beverages like beer. After all, spirits were the type of drink more likely to result in drunken, disorderly behavior. This view seems to have been passed down to the first Texans, since many of their laws placed lesser restrictions on "malt beverages."

Once the talk did turn to prohibition, the country and the state would be divided into clear sides. Drys, or those advocating temperance and eventually prohibition, saw the saloon as the root of all evil. These establishments and the drinks they served bred other vices. They encouraged lewd and immoral behavior, incited lawlessness, destroyed families and lessened the productivity of the American worker. Particularly distasteful to the reformers were red-light districts. Found in most big cities, they were parts of town where corrupt conduct was the norm. Illegal activities within their borders were tolerated or even sanctioned. Law enforcement officers were generally on the take, and it was common for city officials to be invested in the saloons around which these areas were built.

In Dallas, the largest of these was known as Boggy Bayou. This district, "with streets lined by gambling halls, sporting houses and saloons," first developed around the 1870s, south of the intersection of Young and Lamar Streets. Eventually, it would occupy a large portion of southwestern downtown, bounded east to west by Ervay and Houston Streets and north to south by Commerce and Young Streets. By the turn of the century, there were nearly two hundred saloons in Dallas, with a great many located within the confines of this district. Aldermen and a city tax collector owned saloons and bawdyhouses there, and brothels offering all classes of women could be found on virtually every block. In 1904, the city would attempt to corral the "social evil," such that it might not spread across the city, by relocating the bordellos to a more "obscure" spot that would be legally sanctioned with a city ordinance (which was passed in November 1910). The Frogtown district was established in an area that would today be between the Woodall Rodgers Freeway and the American Airlines Center.

Things were even wilder to the immediate west. As author Richard F. Selcer would say in his book bearing the name of Cowtown's notorious red-light district, "Crime and vice in early Fort Worth were virtually synonymous with Hell's Half Acre." You could count on three fingers the "frontier pleasures" that kept the local economy going: drinking, gambling and prostitution. Citizens and politicians tolerated these activities because administering "too stiff a dose of morality…would be bad for business." In the early 1870s, the district's clientele was built around Hell's Half Acre being a regular stop for cattle drives along the Chisolm Trail.

Later, with the coming of the railroad, Fort Worth took on the glow of a western boomtown. A new class of visitor began arriving, and establishments catering to their needs were practically lined up next to each other. One concentration in the 1880s had a set of cribs, essentially one-room brothels, conveniently located on Tenth and Twelfth Streets between the saloons on Main Street and the sporting houses on Rusk Street (now Commerce Street). At its peak, Hell's Half Acre covered the area between Seventh and Fifteenth Streets in one direction and Main and Jones Streets in the other.

Vice centers like Boggy Bayou and Hell's Half Acre were exactly the sort of thing prohibitionists wanted to eliminate. On a more basic level, they believed some people drank too much and were not strong enough to control themselves. In their mind, the only way to cure society's ills was to take away what opponents saw as a basic right. The view of the wets, or anti-prohibitionists, was perhaps best expressed by Oscar Branch Colquitt, governor of Texas from 1911 to 1915. In July of his first year in office, he responded to the question of wet or dry with one of his own: "Is the crime of taking a drink as a beverage so bad as to justify such tyranny? Is all civil liberty and human rights to fall prostrate and be trampled under foot in this way?"

That question, in a nutshell, became the debate. The Bill of Rights to the United States Constitution outlined the liberties and freedoms of an American citizen, yet prohibitionists wanted to see certain freedoms taken away. Who were these people telling others how to live their lives? Was it the government's place to step in and dictate a person's day-to-day choices? The country was about to find out.

TEMPERANCE SENTIMENT may have been strong in those who first came to Texas, but pioneers of the republic were probably more concerned with making a living in a new place than worrying about higher-order social issues. The earliest legislation reflected this attitude, being strictly about generating tax revenue rather than an attempt to institute control measures. In 1837, the Congress of the Republic of Texas passed a law calling for a tax of $100 per year on establishments "retailing wines or spirituous liquors, under one gallon." It was the first liquor law in Texas, and it was notable that those dealing in "cider or malt liquors alone" were not subject to any tax. That stipulation may or may not have been meant to single out liquor peddlers, but a few years later, it was becoming clear that lawmakers were setting their sights on the saloons. Wholesalers were more likely to be selling alcohol by the gallon, whereas saloons were serving patrons in much smaller quantities. Changes in language going forward indicated laws would concentrate on the latter. New guidelines were set for bars, taverns, tippling shops and any other "house of entertainment" where intoxicating liquors were sold in quantities of less than one quart.

In February 1840, Texas's first regulation statute called for such sellers to pay an annual license tax of $250 and to enter into a security bond of $2,500. The bond was to ensure proprietors would "constantly keep a respectable and orderly house" and "prohibit and prevent gaming, quarreling or other misconduct." License applications required approval of the chief justice and were issued to persons "of sufficient probity, and not addicted to any gross immorality." Those unknown to the court could apply and be approved after providing recommendations from three "known and respectable citizens."

Violating conditions of the bond resulted in fines being deducted from the original posting. If the full amount was exhausted, owners could put up a new bond or else be forced to close. By 1910, both numbers had increased gradually to $750 and $5,000, respectively, a development some would suggest pointed to the "growth of temperance sentiment among the people of Texas."

Further legislation proposed in 1854 seeking to close the saloons resulted in the first liquor election in Texas. The law was local option in nature, whereby neighborhood shops would be closed on August 8, 1854, unless a majority of citizens voted to license such establishments in their particular county. A day ahead of the effective date, forty-one counties went to the polls and reported results to the secretary of state. Of these, only seven voted "for license." Enforcement was delayed due to a constitutional challenge, and the law was repealed in 1856, presumably for the same reason. Even so, poll results were seen as a foreshadowing of how local option elections would shake out in the future.

From there, regulation at the local level manifested itself in the so-called schoolhouse prohibition laws. Between 1854 and 1875, roughly 150 communities turned to the state to enact laws prohibiting the sale of intoxicating liquors within a set distance of certain types of buildings. (Most included exemptions for sacramental or medicinal purposes.) In Fort Worth, sales were outlawed within four and a half miles of the courthouse in December 1861, while in Dallas, such businesses were banned "within five miles of town" as of December 1863. A year later, similar controls were put in place around the courthouse in Waxahachie. After 1869, the most commonly named structures were schools and seminaries once a provision granting the legislature power to restrict sales in their proximity was included in the Texas Constitution. A Masonic institute in Grapevine was among those that would be protected, along with a high school in Collin County.

Well over fifty laws of this type were requested and passed between 1870 and 1875, meaning they were taking up a good bit of the legislature's time. An amendment to the state constitution would be proposed to ease the burden and transfer jurisdiction to the local level.

EBENEEZER "EBEN" LAFAYETTE DOHONEY, whom the *Paris News* called "the father of Prohibition in Texas," gave the first speech on local option in the South after announcing his candidacy for the Texas Constitutional Convention of 1875. He was elected as a delegate, after which he authored a resolution to include local option in the constitution. Dohoney did not introduce it himself but instead appealed to a Baptist preacher to do so after having been labeled "a prohibitionist crank." It remained buried in committee for three months before he was able to convince the members "it did not commit the state to prohibition" but instead "adopted the good old democratic doctrine of self-government." By the time the resolution came up for debate, it was late in the session, and many lawmakers had already gone home. The provision was added with surprisingly little resistance, and the constitution itself was adopted on February 15, 1876.

Later that year, the first local-option election in Texas was held in Jasper County on December 8. Drys won the day by a margin of only fourteen votes. The North Texas county of Rockwall was soon to follow, while others would vote dry only to go back to being wet again in future elections. A decade later, Jones County was the only other county besides Jasper and Rockwall that remained dry leading up to Texas's first attempt to enact prohibition at the state level in 1887.

The idea of statewide prohibition came about due to the fact that local option was a piecemeal solution at best. Although it solved the problem of Congress having to draft special legislation to enact things like schoolhouse prohibition, local option was not a path toward widespread reform. Even if a county or precinct went dry, the next one over might be wet, meaning liquor was still readily available. It was also all too easy to call a new vote based on a change in sentiment, reversing the results of the previous year. Overall, the belief was that statewide prohibition based on constitutional amendment would wipe out the saloons once and for all, and it had a better chance of long-term success.

Reformers from outside the state would play a role in getting the issue into the hands of the voters. One was Dr. James Younge, a lecturer who organized the United Friends of Temperance (UFT) after relocating to Texas in 1869. According to co-worker Harry Haynes, Younge spent the next eighteen years as a "white plume at the head of the column that stimulated our purpose." The UFT was a secret fraternity and the first statewide temperance organization. Haynes identified the group's goals to be complete abstinence on the part of the membership and total prohibition throughout the state.

The UFT's approach was said to have evolved from moral suasion in the 1860s to agitation in the 1880s. Regardless of how the group went about it, it was able to get a statewide prohibition amendment submitted to the Texas legislature in 1881. The effort was unsuccessful despite gaining Senate approval, prompting UFT leaders to suggest anti-prohibitionist money was responsible for it being stranded in the House of Representatives.

Around this same time, another well-known temperance advocate was active in the state supporting prohibition and women's rights. Frances E. Willard was the president of the Woman's Christian Temperance Union (WCTU), an organization whose goals mirrored those of the UFT. The WCTU grew out of a "Woman's Crusade" that began in a small Ohio town, where women protested alcohol's evils by kneeling down in praying bands outside local saloons.

Willard first visited Texas in May 1881 with the help of Dohoney. The Texas reformer arranged for Willard to appear at an opera house near his home in Paris after a local church refused to allow her access. He assisted Willard once again when she returned for a tour of sixteen Texas communities beginning in February 1882. The goal of Willard's tour was to organize local chapters of the WCTU. As she progressed through the state, she lectured to large and enthusiastic crowds in every town. By the time she left, sixteen unions had formed, and there were plans to form a state organization. The number of unions grew to around one hundred within a few years, resulting in women being given the unprecedented opportunity to have an active role with a high level of visibility in public service. Willard's visit galvanized temperance efforts, leading to a flurry of local-option elections both during and after her tour.

6
ONWARD TO PROHIBITION
(1887–1919)

Many businesses, especially saloons, closed their doors on August 4, 1887, the day statewide prohibition was submitted to the voting public for the first time. In many cities, the WCTU set up outside polling places to hand out food and drink to voters. It and the UFT had been instrumental in the effort to get to this point. Eben Dohoney had been as well, moving on from a failed Texas congressional bid in 1882 to serve alongside Frances Willard at the Prohibition Party's National Convention in 1884. On September 8 of that year, he called for a meeting of prohibitionists in Fort Worth to gather votes for the national party's ticket in the upcoming presidential election. After two years, he found himself representing the Prohibition Party of Texas as its candidate for governor. His nomination came during the first Prohibition Party Convention of Texas, which convened in Dallas on September 7, 1886. He garnered only 19,186 votes in losing to Lawrence Sullivan Ross, a Democrat and anti-prohibitionist.

These activities and the growing influence of the Prohibition Party caught the attention of the then-dominant Democrats, who agreed to submit a proposal for statewide prohibition after initially refusing to consider it a year earlier. The text of the proposed amendment presented to the voters was straightforward and to the point: "The manufacture, sale and exchange of intoxicating liquors except for medicinal, mechanical, sacramental and scientific purposes, is hereby prohibited in the State of Texas." The amendment met with a resounding defeat. A total of 349,827 votes were cast: 129,270 for and 220,627 against. Wet had won with a 91,357-vote majority.

Breaking down the election, only 32 out of 187 Texas counties voted for prohibition. Except for Fannin, Cooke, Tarrant and Williamson, most counties voting for the amendment were sparsely populated. Residents of Dallas County, the most populous in the state at the time, were against it by a nearly two-to-one margin. Of the major cities, only Fort Worth sided with the dry vote. There, speculation arose that the result was influenced by the sensational murder of Michael Haggerty, killed a few weeks ahead of the election by W.T. Grigsby, proprietor of the Unique Saloon. The two men were friends, and Haggerty approached Grigsby in an effort to calm him during an apparent fit of drunken rage. A doctor attending the killer just after the incident confirmed that suspicion, declaring Grigsby's behavior to be the result of alcohol delirium.

With news of the defeat, members of the WCTU recommitted themselves and were back to work within days of the election. However, for the UFT, it was a deathblow. It ceased to exist as a statewide organization, with members choosing the divide-and-conquer approach offered by local option. It went beyond just the UFT as prohibitionists in general placed a renewed focus on local option after the election. From there, it was a county-by-county, precinct-by-precinct fight for the next twenty years. For a time, the reformers literally grasped small victories from the jaws of their 1887 defeat. Between 1893 and 1903 alone, roughly 140 counties and hundreds of precincts went dry. This included most of North Texas outside the larger cities of Dallas and Fort Worth.

These inroads led to the formation of the Texas Brewers Association (TBA) in February 1901. A joint agreement suggested the group's purpose was nothing more than a way to present a united front in the face of labor disputes: "The object of this organization is to strengthen the hands of the individual brewery in making its labor contracts, to ensure uniformity of such contracts and to effectually support the industry affected by any strike or boycott." Membership consisted of the Dallas Brewery, Texas Brewing Company of Fort Worth, Galveston Brewing Company, Houston Ice and Brewing Company, San Antonio Brewing Association, American Brewing Association of Houston, Lone Star Brewing Company of San Antonio, Anheuser-Busch, Willam J. Lemp and Frederick Pabst.

Not surprisingly, the association's attention quickly focused on the issue of prohibition. One of its first orders of business was to lobby against a proposed amendment to the state constitution requiring poll tax receipts be shown prior to a person being allowed to vote. The concern dated back to the overwhelming anti-prohibitionist sentiment shown by African

Americans and immigrants in the past. In effect, the passage of the law would disenfranchise people in these groups because they simply could not afford to pay the tax. Despite the efforts of the TBA, voters in Texas approved the measure in December 1902.

Brewers also came up short in their support of a 1903 bill that would have slowed the momentum of local-option elections. The measure sought to institute a two-year waiting period between votes, something that would have eased the constant pressure of prohibitionists who worked to call new elections as often and in as many counties as possible. The brewers' frustration with local option in general can be seen in a letter sent from Dallas Brewery president Samuel T. Morgan to the San Antonio Brewing Association: "From recent results it would seem that the Prohibition cause will have to run its course before we can hope to carry very many of the elections. The people have simply gone wild, and it will take time to let them see the error of their way."

Prohibitionists recognized a response was needed to the growing pressure of organizations like the TBA to build upon gains realized over the prior decade. One group that emerged to counter the brewers was the Texas Local Option Association (TLOA). It outlined its goals in a November 1903 meeting: "The purpose…is to associate the local option organizations now existing and hereafter…in a state organization to the end that a campaign of education as to the evils of the liquor traffic may be more effectually and economically carried on in Texas."

Both the brewers and the TLOA took up the cause at the county and precinct levels. The TLOA sent representatives to speak and provide guidance on local-option elections. Brewers approached things a different way. Between 1903 and 1911, they employed a man named Paget to act as an agent for the association. His instructions amounted to finding ways to prevent, control or otherwise influence elections for the betterment of the brewers. He was also tasked with paying poll taxes for individuals believed to be sympathetic to their way of thinking.

Over the five-year period between 1903 and 1908, it was a virtual stalemate between the two sides. Counties would be won and lost, though drys did maintain an advantage at the precinct level. The suddenly stagnant progress had prohibitionists eyeing a statewide amendment once again. Before another attempt at that, lawmakers passed a number of measures aimed at cleaning up the saloons. One was proposed by Democrats T.H. McGregor of Austin and Albert Baskin Sr. of Fort Worth. Adopted in April 1907, the Baskin-McGregor Act called for retail liquor sellers to obtain a license and required them to pay an occupation tax of $375 in addition to posting a $5,000 bond. If there was any doubt the law targeted saloons, one only need look at the fees charged to individuals dealing exclusively in malt liquors. For them, the cost was only $62.50 with a $1,000 bond.

The provisions of the law were detailed and far-reaching. Licenses were forfeited if a business was found to have sold alcohol to minors, allowed the presence of "prostitutes or lewd women" or permitted illegal gaming. Establishments were to close on Sunday and at midnight on all other days. Women could not be employed as servers or bartenders unless they were a member of the owner's family, and none was allowed to work as a dancer or singer—not that having entertainers would have mattered much, considering a "piano, organ or other musical instrument" could not be on the grounds for any reason whatsoever. You also could not play cards, dominoes or dice, and you were not allowed to have a bowling alley or billiard table.

Exhibitions of boxing, wrestling and cock fighting were off-limits as well. It would have hardly been worth the trouble, anyway, as having any of these activities might cause you to overstep the quiet clause, which held saloonkeepers accountable should your voice be heard by a passerby on the street. Basically, you could purchase and enjoy a drink on the premises with no entertainment and no interaction with women who were not related to the proprietor—unless your wife, mother, daughter or sister notified a peace officer in writing that you were not to be served in the first place. Violations resulted in fines or imprisonment for the proprietor.

Although it would be July 1907 before the Baskin-McGregor Act went into effect, Fort Worth began enforcement in April after including the features of the bill in a charter to switch over to a commission form of government. In a warning to saloonkeepers, Mayor W.D. Harris declared, "I fully believe that these new laws will effectually solve the liquor problem." In September, the TBA came out in support of the legislation and even offered its help. A letter addressed to the public in September 1907 pledged to give prosecutors "aid financially or otherwise, to assist in the fullest enforcement of the Baskin-McGregor law." It was nearly identical to a message the group had circulated in early 1904 under the guise of seeking to "purify the liquor traffic" and preserve the "good name of the brewing industry."

The TBA would eventually gain an ally in the Retail Liquor Dealers Association in 1907, but that same year saw the formation of a more formidable opponent in the Anti-Saloon League (ASL) of Texas. Headquartered in Dallas, the ASL proceeded to assimilate groups like the

TLOA into its structure. It was nonpartisan with a singular focus, and its arrival was seen as a boost to prohibition efforts in the state.

A Democratic primary was held in July 1908 to gauge opinion on whether an amendment for statewide prohibition should be submitted to the legislature later that year. A total of 286,571 votes were cast, resulting in a 4,089 majority for submission. Only three North Texas counties voted against it, those being Dallas, Palo Pinto and Tarrant County. Based on the result, Democrats demanded submission of an amendment as part of their party platform, whereas Republicans opposed it as part of theirs. When it came up for consideration in Congress, the legislature failed to obtain the required two-thirds majority. As was the case in 1881, when a similar amendment failed to make it through the House, prohibitionists believed the well-funded liquor interests were to blame.

To the dismay of the liquor industry, the issue was quickly raised again. A new primary was held in 1910, resulting in a greater majority for submission. The legislature responded to the call, and a referendum for state prohibition was held in July 1911; nearly a half million people went to the polls. Drys would come up short again, but the margin was far less than it had been in 1887. The final tally was 231,096 for and 237,393 against; the measure was defeated by only 6,297 votes. Once more, liquor money was singled out as the cause by the drys, more specifically, funds provided by the brewers to assist African Americans. They were most likely referring to the payment of poll taxes. Suffrage was still an issue, but even if a fraction of the more than 150,000 African American men over the age of twenty-one were able to cast a ballot, it would have been enough to sway the election.

In 1915, the State of Texas would take a closer look at these and other tactics being utilized by the TBA in the political arena. Referencing legislation passed in April 1907, the state would accuse brewers of misusing "corporate funds, means and assets in unlawful attempts to affect, influence or control the results of elections in Texas and to affect and influence legislation both state and national." According to attorney general B.F. Looney, the allegations represented a systematic abuse of power over a period of twelve years. Not surprisingly, this time period coincided with much of the time Paget was employed by the brewers to carry out his specialized duties.

Originally, brewers were part of a suit against the Texas Business Men's Association. This booster organization was effectively Texas's first statewide chamber of commerce. It allegedly used contributions to engage in an extensive campaign aimed at swaying public sentiment on political issues by way of pamphlets, newspaper articles and other forms of the printed word. While building the case against that group, the state uncovered a more wide-ranging effort by brewers to enlist the aid of others in their fight against prohibition. One such letter in evidence from Adolphus Busch to Texas Brewing Company president Zane-Cetti reads: "We must pay over to the United States Brewing Association whatever it may require to represent us properly before congress, where we have most important bills to defend. We must defeat that Hepburn-Dolliver bill, which is most dangerous and antagonistic to our industry and which makes prohibition possible."

The Hepburn-Dolliver bill, which did not pass, was of particular concern to Busch and other wholesalers. Its purpose was to make alcoholic beverages "transported into any state…subject to the operation and effect of the laws of such state." At the time, interstate shipments were exempt from any prohibition laws that existed in the state that received them.

On the local level, insight into the role of the TBA can be found in the text of a contract agreed to by its members: "The undersigned hereby agree to pay an assessment of 20 (twenty) cents per barrel on their sales of keg beer in Texas, and 1 (one) cent per dozen of bottle beer…to be spent by a committee to be appointed by and under the direction of the subscribers for the purpose of promoting anti-prohibition matters in Texas." According to the state's charge, this was the money used to influence elections as well as to pay "poll taxes to qualify persons known to such parties to have views… favorable to the legalizing of the sale of intoxicating liquors."

All together, the state spent the better part of 1915 taking testimony and compiling twenty-five volumes of evidence containing around twenty-five thousand documents and weighing over five hundred pounds. Once the dust settled in January 1916, six breweries went the route of compromise, agreeing as they did in the 1901 antitrust case to reduced fines and forfeiture of their charters in exchange for a plea of guilty. The lone holdout was the Dallas Brewery, which admitted to making contributions to affect local-option elections prior to 1907 but argued that such activities were not illegal at the time. The court agreed, resulting in the brewery being subject to a lesser fine of only $5,000. Adding that and the Texas Brewing Company's liability of $14,000 to the final tally, penalties aggregating $276,000 were collected by the state. New charters were filed, putting the breweries back in business, but the cloud of prohibition was showing no signs of dissipation.

ALTHOUGH TEXAS WAS NOT AMONG THEM, eight other states had enacted statewide prohibition by 1911. However, like the limitations that had been realized regarding local option in counties and precincts, there was a growing belief that trying to reform the country state by state would have minimal impact as well. To that end, efforts gradually shifted toward instituting prohibition at the national level.

For that to happen, the federal government needed a way to offset the loss of tax revenue attributable to alcohol sales. The means would be the Sixteenth Amendment to the United States Constitution. Adopted on February 3, 1913, it allowed Congress to collect a personal income tax. Estimates of total government revenue were in the neighborhood of $700 million in 1911. A little less than half of that came from taxes on tobacco, spirits and other items. The income tax was expected to generate approximately $100 million in revenue, helping to fill the gap that would be left with the removal of alcohol.

With that resolved, the final push toward a national ban came as a result of World War I. The United States declared war on Germany on April 6, 1917. There was some belief that German Americans supported the Central Powers prior to the declaration, but there is ample evidence to suggest that most sided with the United States once it entered the war. Of course, some of the largest breweries in America were owned by German Americans, but they, too, showed their support. The son of Gustav Pabst and the grandson of Adolphus Busch enlisted in the armed forces, while the Busch family contributed $500,000 to the war effort, and brewers from Milwaukee and their employees purchased $2 million in Liberty Bonds. Still, anti-German propaganda and national Anti-Saloon League efforts to connect German brewers to treasonous activities were enough to sway public sentiment toward the prohibitionist side.

Making matters worse for brewers, President Woodrow Wilson called for the passage of a wartime food control bill in 1917. The Anti-Saloon League tried to seize the opportunity and lobbied to outlaw the use of grain in the manufacture of alcoholic beverages, but Congress pushed through a compromise with only a ban on distilled liquors. Wilson, though, reserved the right to put similar measures in place for beer and wine at a later time. He did just that in December 1917, cutting grain usage in beer and wine by 30 percent and reducing the allowable alcohol content to 2.75 percent by weight. Soon after, over half of the country's breweries would go out of business. The rest would effectively be shuttered in September of the following year after crop failures and a labor shortage prompted the president to cut off brewery supplies completely.

The Eighteenth Amendment to the United States Constitution ensured they would be shut down for good. Authored by Morris Sheppard, a senator from Texarkana, it was ratified on January 16, 1919. The Volstead Act would follow in October, establishing the ways in which the amendment would be enforced. In the meantime, Texas finally managed to pass a statewide prohibition amendment in May with a 20,075-vote majority. National Prohibition took effect on January 17, 1920. The nation's "Noble Experiment" had begun.

ESTIMATES ON THE IMPACT of Prohibition were being made long before it became a reality. In Dallas, "one brewery, twelve wholesale liquor houses, and 203 saloons" would close on the day the law went into effect and as many as 1,500 people would lose their jobs. Samuel T. Morgan, president of the Dallas Brewery, said his business would be converted to an ice plant, likely meaning some or all of his workers would be spared. He sounded less than optimistic when he followed that up with the assessment that "there are too many of such concerns in Dallas already." Fort Worth had its brewery too, along with around 10 liquor houses and over 150 saloons. Other businesses in both cities and across the state would feel the effects as well, a short list of which might include cooperage works, box makers, grain suppliers and others.

Over the years, many advertisements for the Texas Brewing Company included statements that highlighted its importance to the local economy. Even though the point was subtler, most of the time they were referring to what would be lost with Prohibition. Other times, like in a 1903 ad, the message was decidedly more direct:

> *This institution pays one-fiftieth of the total taxes of Fort Worth.*
> *Distributes fifty thousand dollars annually among the merchants of Fort Worth for merchandise bought here.*
> *Pays one hundred and twenty-five thousand dollars in wages, every dollar of which is spent in the city.*
> *Furnishes directly the support of one-fiftieth of Fort Worth's population.*
> *Uses its profits in betterments and extension of the plant.*
> *Encourages home industry to the utmost limit.*
> *Until the advent of the packing houses, it was Fort Worth's largest industrial enterprise.*
> *INDISCRIMINATE PROHIBITION THREATENS ITS EXISTENCE.*

While the fate of wholesalers and saloon owners was clear, all was not lost for brewery workers. Business models did change for both North Texas breweries, but neither shut down completely. Brewery-specific functions that were no longer needed might have resulted in lost jobs, but the whole of the workforce was not destined to be left out on the street.

The Dallas Brewery altered its original post-Prohibition plan and became the Grain Juice Company, maker of a non-intoxicating "pure cereal and hop beverage" called Graino. It was probably similar to Malt Wein, a malt-extract product the brewery produced in the early 1900s that was bolstered with the "strengthening and tonic properties of health giving hops." Graino, it claimed, had been a success in western markets for a number of years. Whether it was or not, the company was unable to stay in business as a soft drink manufacturer.

In 1925, much of the site was cleared for new construction associated with a name change to the Morgan Warehouse and Industrial Company. The new direction called for the business to "act as manufacturing agents and distributors for groceries, beverages and soda fountain supplies." Through it all, Samuel T. Morgan and principal investor Thomas Keeley remained as constants—that is until Morgan, who had been with the company as secretary and then president since Keeley acquired it in 1893, passed away in January 1928. Just two and a half years later, the last remnants of the old Dallas Brewery were torn down to make room for further expansion of the firm.

The Texas Brewing Company prepared for the next phase of its existence by making a $300,000 investment in the construction of additional cold storage capacity. Its new venture was first called the Texas Beverage and Cold Storage Company, then the Texas Ice and Refrigerating Company after a reincorporation in 1922. Almost symbolically, then-president and one of the original founders of the brewery in Fort Worth, Jesse Shenton Zane-Cetti, passed away in February 1922.

With Prohibition, the deaths of Morgan and Zane-Cetti and the demolition of the Dallas Brewery building, North Texas's first brewing era had come to an end. Eventually, beer would be brewed again, both at the corner of Jones and Ninth Streets in Fort Worth and on the old, original location of the Dallas Brewery. It would be soon for one and much later for the other.

7
REPEAL AND REBIRTH
(1920–1938)

In no uncertain terms, Prohibition was a failure. Those who disagreed with the law simply defied it; some turned to homebrewing, while others took up more illicit pursuits. Cities became breeding grounds for crime and corruption, all for want of a drink. Enforcement was essentially impossible, and a government eager to prove it could keep criminals in line had to get creative with civil liberties to make examples out of those who broke the law. As Stanley Baron put it in *Brewed in America: A History of Beer and Ale in the United States*: "The Volstead Act is a classic example of a law so unpopular with the general public that it cannot be enforced except at a huge expense and by measures that come close to abrogating constitutional rights."

Local agencies were struggling almost immediately. In September 1920, a Prohibition inspector assigned to Dallas noted, "The violation of the national prohibition law in Dallas seems to be on the incline rather than the decrease." Another inspector based in Fort Worth stated his officers were filing an average of four charges per day. Indeed, headlines calling attention to seizures were commonplace in area newspapers, and the never-ending reports were evidence that law enforcement efforts were not really putting a stop to anything. Bootleggers roamed free in April 1922, at least according to Texas governor Pat M. Neff, who accused Dallas mayor Sawnie R. Aldredge of dropping the ball on enforcement. The relative ease of obtaining black-market booze led one writer to refer to the city as "dripping dry Dallas."

North Texans were getting their hands on spirits like whiskey and gin, as well as a concoction called "choc beer." This potent liquor made from blackstrap molasses, corn pone, yeast and water could have an alcohol percentage of over 20. You could even get a kick from flavored extracts, something readily available from a perfectly legitimate source. One Texas grocer described a process by which you could "cut a cup-shaped hole in a cake of ice and fill it with extract. In just a minute or two the lemon content, which is a syrup, becomes thick and gummy from the cold." Because alcohol does not freeze, it was easily separated from the muck and poured off into a glass.

The government simply lacked the funds necessary to provide enough field agents to police the rumrunners, bootleggers, gangsters and speakeasies, not to mention any number of other small-time violators. Congressional appropriations went from $6 million in 1921 to $16 million in 1932, and it was still not enough. The ever-increasing amounts flew in the face of the idea that the federal income tax would help fill the void left in the national treasury by alcohol revenues. It might have if not for millions upon millions of dollars being directed toward enforcement.

States were on the hook as well, and with no means of replacing their own alcohol tax revenue, they were basically being bled dry. What used to be saloon money was now being put in the pockets of the bootleggers and those who ran the speakeasies rather than back into the local economy. If lawmakers needed any more reason to repeal Prohibition, the final straw had to be the Great Depression. The government needed money, and people needed work. What better way to stock the treasury and create jobs than to reestablish a lost industry?

With that, the end came in stages. Texas voted to ratify the Twenty-first Amendment to the United States Constitution in August 1933. The results were effective after ninety days, making Texas the thirty-second state to repeal the Eighteenth Amendment on November 24, 1933. However, it was another vote in the same election that got breweries back in business. Voters approved an amendment to Article XVI, Section 20 of the Texas Constitution allowing the sale of beer and wine not exceeding 3.2 percent alcohol by weight. It matched the principles of the Cullen-Harrison Act, a prerequisite bill the United States Congress had enacted in March. Without this amendment, breweries in Texas would have still been in a state of limbo because the state's own prohibition law was still in effect. That portion of Section 20 was amended after a vote in August 1935. The 3.2 percent provision remained, but like its wet/dry status, each political subdivision could determine on its own whether to allow alcoholic beverages of greater strength.

When the switch was flipped and Prohibition turned into a new beginning, more than a few businessmen were entertaining thoughts of opening a brewery. The principals of the old Dallas Brewery were among them, claiming for months ahead of repeal that they intended to get back in the game. Henry K. Maas, now general manager of the Morgan Warehouse and Commercial Company, said in November 1932 that land had been reserved for the building of a new brewery in the event that beer would again be legalized. They also took care to preserve the wells that were once used to supply water to the old facility. By the August 1933 vote to allow 3.2 percent beer, the decision was made to function solely as a distributor instead of a manufacturer of alcohol. For that purpose, the Keeley Brewing Company of Texas was formed by the same officers but as a separate entity from Morgan Warehouse. Later that year, Morgan Warehouse began selling beer for the Kingsbury Brewing Company of Wisconsin.

Maas explained the company's decision in a September 1933 interview. Although the idea of rebuilding the brewery had not been abandoned, they believed it would be difficult to round up investors to the tune of $750,000. Likely referencing the fact that the state's prohibition law had not yet been fully repealed, he stated one of the reasons was the fear that beer would again be made illegal. Beyond that, he spoke of local option and how its impact meant the likelihood of reduced demand given the large number of dry counties adjacent to Dallas.

Others exploring breweries in North Texas were outside investors with money to spend. One was described as "a wealthy American distiller and brewer in Mexico." Due to the difficult business environment south of the border, he wanted to close down his plants there and build a $2 million brewery in Texas. Another was a businessman from Omaha, Nebraska, who envisioned a $1 million plant capable of producing seventy-five thousand barrels per year. He even went so far as to option a seventy-three-acre tract of land just outside Fort Worth for what was to be called the Southwest Brewing Company. A third, more modest proposal from a San Antonio capitalist looked to build a $175,000 facility at the corner of Orange and Cochran Streets in Dallas. Unfortunately, none of these projects ever got off the ground, and in the case of the Dallas Brewery site, over fifty years would pass before beer would be brewed there again. The proverbial light at the end of the tunnel was to the west, where a former brewery was being brought back to life.

THE FIRST NORTH TEXAS BREWERY to emerge after Prohibition was the Superior Brewing Company of Fort Worth. In the summer of 1933,

President and brewmaster Oscar Lamsens (white suit and tie in front row, third from the left) stands with the employees of the Superior Brewing Company. *From the collection of Barbara Lamsens.*

workers began remodeling the old Texas Brewing Company plant at Jones and Ninth Streets in anticipation of the passage of the 3.2 percent beer law. The building was leased from the Texas Ice and Refrigerating Company, the business that had evolved from the original brewery shortly after the onset of Prohibition. Superior would also contract with its landlords for all of the brewery's cold storage needs.

Plans called for the installation of new brewing and bottling equipment costing $50,000. Once completed, the capacity of the rejuvenated plant was expected to be 2,400 cases per day. The principal investors were Sam Leiter, formerly of St. Louis, and longtime brewer Oscar Lamsens. They chartered the company and had their first product on the market by October 1933. The "new Texas beer brewed by an old Belgian *braumeister*" was simply called Superior Beer and sold for $2 per case in July of the following year.

Lamsens, who was also the president of the company, had been in the brewing industry for thirty years. His first exposure to the business had come at a brewery founded by his father in Brussels, Belgium. Despite his father's death when Lamsens was just three years old, the brewery had grown and was still in operation, taken over and run by his eventual stepfather. Lamsens was still a part owner of that establishment, but he spent the early part of his own career working as a brewmaster in Flanders. It was around that time that he studied under a man named Frantz Brogniez, presumably at a brewing school started by the latter in Lichtervelde. Brogniez, who would one day work in Texas at the Houston Ice and Brewing Company, first came to the United States in 1896. Shortly thereafter, he would start what became the Tivoli Brewing Company of Detroit, and it was there that Lamsens would work after immigrating to the United States around 1900. This was prior to plying his trade at that city's American Brewing Company up until Prohibition.

Also on Lamsens's resume was the development of a patented carbonation method called the Lamsens Process. What differentiated it from other approaches at the time was that it force-carbonated beer by way of a submerged "comminuting chamber." This apparatus had walls made of a porous material, allowing injected gas to be transferred to the beer through microscopic holes. These "infinitesimal bubbles" afforded "the most intimate contact with the beer," resulting in a "simple and natural" carbonation process.

At Superior, Lamsens was joined in the day-to-day operation of the brewery by his son, Orlando, the vice-president and assistant brewer, along with Dan E. Curtis, who started out as the secretary-treasurer of the firm but later assumed the title of manager. Curtis and Lamsens gave occasional business updates to the *Fort Worth Star-Telegram*, which provided an additional promotional vehicle to go with the brewery's modest newspaper advertisements. Their minimalistic approach may have been the result of work done by the brewery to determine how best to promote its beer: "During the past two years the organization has made extensive surveys as to the best methods of advertising the good qualities of Superior beer and to determine just what types of flavors of beer are most popular, with the result that…customers were by far their best salesman."

The brewery reported increasing demand throughout its distribution area in 1935, with Lamsens being "especially pleased…with the increase locally, which proves a high degree of loyalty on the part of Fort Worth." Despite the statements of growth, court documents related to *Superior Brewing Co. v. Curtis* indicate all was not well with the brewery behind the scenes. Heard by the Court of Civil Appeals of Texas in April 1938, the case involved a dispute over unpaid salary Curtis claimed he was due after resigning his position in

February 1936. In the written opinion, which affirmed a lower court decision in favor of Curtis, it was noted that a meeting of the stockholders was held in January 1935 regarding "problems facing the corporation" caused by "dissension and lack of co-operation" within its ranks. Salaries were cut to reduce expenses, but the brewery was still unable to turn a profit.

The year 1935, which saw Superior introduce a new beer called Prosit Golden Lager, was the most visible for the brewery in terms of advertising. Afterward, outside of a seasonal bock release in February 1936 and ads for a new pilsner in 1938, the brewery stayed relatively quiet. It remained that way throughout the rest of the decade until November 1940, when Oscar Lamsens passed away while working at the brewery. The business folded soon after. Other food-related businesses would occupy space among the buildings at Jones and Ninth Streets over the years, but they were vacant in 1973 when the site was razed to "modernize and beautify sections of the city's core." Today the area is home to the Fort Worth Intermodal Transportation Center.

8
DALLAS IN THE POST-PROHIBITION ERA (1934–1941)

Among the many names that have been a part of the city's past, Schepps is one of the most well known in the history of Dallas. Most are more likely to associate it with milk than beer, but once upon a time, the family name was attached to the first post-Prohibition brewery in Dallas. It was built by brothers George and Julius Schepps, and it makes for an interesting side note in the lives and legacies of the two men.

George would say in a 1981 interview with *D Magazine* that Julius was the philanthropist. The older of the two, Julius went on to become a well-respected Jewish civic leader who contributed time and money to countless organizations in Dallas during his lifetime. A freeway and park are named in his honor: The Julius Schepps Highway runs along Interstate 45, between Interstate 20 and Interstate 30, southeast of downtown Dallas. Just north and west of where the road changes over to U.S. 75 sits Julius Schepps Park. It occupies a 9,300-square-foot slice of greenbelt along Commerce Street east of North Cesar Chavez Boulevard. There stands a 9-foot-tall bronze statue of the man, commissioned by the Schepps family and the City of Dallas, created by artist Michael Pavlovsky and dedicated in 2002.

The swinger, as George characterized himself, was a well-documented philanthropist in his own right, who spent much of his life involved in amateur athletics. He coached different sports at the semi-pro level but may have had his greatest success with a girls' basketball team that won a national American Athletic Union title in 1929. His first love, though, was baseball. Seventeen years after he guided a team made up of employees from his father's bakery to a city championship, he bought his first minor league baseball team in 1938, one of seven he owned in the time after World War II. In 1978, he established the Texas Baseball Hall of Fame, and he is often referred to as one of the state's baseball pioneers.

Their parents were Russian immigrants, Joe and Jennie Schepps, coming to America in 1890 and eventually settling and opening their bakery in Dallas around 1901. George and Julius delivered newspapers and worked at the family business, with Julius taking over and running it after their father died in 1922. It was sold in 1928, but the family lost money in the stock market crash the following year. To pay off debts, the brothers partnered in an insurance agency, something Julius stayed involved with for over forty years. As for George, he sold his interest after Prohibition and turned his attention to beer.

In November 1933, Schepps Superior Beer Distributors was incorporated with capital stock of $1,000 for the purposes of marketing Schepps' own brand of beer. It would be brewed by the Superior Brewing Company of Fort Worth under the supervision of brewmaster Oscar Lamsens. Conforming to the prevailing 3.2 percent beer law, Schepps Superior Beer was described as "neutral tasting" and "said to be the happy medium between hoppy and sweet." It probably had what George referred to as a "clean taste," based on how he described his own preferences to the interviewer in 1981: "Just as soon as it hits the palate, my taste buds should taste nothing that's resentful to me. I actually force myself to burp to see if I get an aftertaste. And if I don't, well, that sho' is fine beer."

Just three months later, George was back in the news with plans to spend $200,000 to build the family's own brewery in Dallas. The Schepps Brewing Corporation would sell beer in bottles and kegs, but the company planned to continue handling products for Superior until construction of the new facility was complete. A lease was secured on a two-story building located at 1026 Young Street in March 1934. Both brothers were listed as incorporators on the original charter, and it was noted upon opening that the brewery was wholly owned by Dallas stockholders. Julius's son Phil joined as brewmaster in 1937 after attending the Siebel Institute of Technology in Chicago. This was after Julius had moved on to establish the Julius Schepps Company in 1935, a longtime liquor wholesaler in the city, and before George left in early 1939 to concentrate on his newly purchased Dallas Giants baseball club.

Phil stayed on until the brewery was reorganized under a different name in 1939, which ended up being only a few months after George's

Employees of the Schepps Brewing Corporation gather prior to a Labor Day parade in 1937. *From the Schepps family collection.*

resignation. A comment Phil made in 1978 may provide some insight into why the family eventually left the business. He said Schepps Xtra, the brewery's best-selling beer, was unable to make a profit in the face of competition from the larger national brands. It was on the lighter side, something George thought would appeal to a younger generation more inclined to drink beers with less bitterness. In terms of pricing, it was only $1.75, compared to a dollar more for Budweiser and Coors. The store running the ad explained the lower price of Schepps as, "Not a cheap beer, but sold at this price because it's made in Dallas and you do not have to pay any transportation charges."

At its peak, the brewery produced around 100,000 barrels per year. Brands like Schepps Beer, the brewery's first product, were "leisurely aged" in vats made of solid redwood. In addition to Schepps Xtra, other products included Schepps Old Fashioned Ale, Stein-Gold and others. The last of these was packaged in a short and squat twelve-ounce "steinie bottle" with a permanently embossed label. Seasonal brews were also offered—Schepps Bock Beer was touted as "the treat of the season" in an ad selling cases for $1.98 in March 1935. A year later, the brewery rolled out Schepps Summer Xtra, a beer that was "brewed in Texas to fit Texas weather."

Decades later, while working as president for the Julius Schepps Company, Phil tried to revive the Schepps beer brand by partnering with Spoetzel Brewery in Shiner to brew Schepps Xtra Light Lager in 1978. There were a number of other light beers on the market at the time, which may account for the use of the term "light" in the modern version. According to Phil, it was just a word and not meant to suggest the beer was low in calories or alcohol. "Nostalgia and the family's ego were the top two" reasons for attempting the comeback, he said, with profits coming in a close third. Ultimately, the new beer failed to catch on.

The Schepps family name continued to be prominent in North Texas into the new millennium. George and Phil both worked in some capacity for the Julius Schepps Company, which became one of the largest independent liquor wholesalers in the country. It operated under that name until it was acquired by Republic Beverages in 1991. There was also the Schepps Dairy, which Joe Schepps's brother, Nathan, started in 1915. That company was later run by Nathan's sons Harmon and Eli, who assumed control in the early 1940s. The dairy business was sold in 1985, eventually changing hands a number of times before becoming a subsidiary of Dean Foods. In 2010, Dean announced plans to phase out the Schepps name in favor of the Oak Farms label.

Today, the park bearing Julius Schepps's name is steps from where his wholesale liquor company did business at 2305 Canton Street. The brewery was just blocks away on Young Street, located on the grounds now occupied by Dallas City Hall Plaza.

PLANS FOR A SECOND BREWERY to be located in Dallas were unveiled in April 1934, just two months after Schepps had gone public with its announcement. Superior Brewing Company stockholder Sam Leiter and partner Charles F. Kruse, who, like Leiter, had moved from St. Louis, took out a lease on the old William J. Lemp bottling plant at 311 Dundee and Pacific Streets. (Located at present-day Malcolm X Boulevard and Indiana Street, this building was on the same block as the main office of Lemp's facility on Crowdus Street.) Remodeling costs on the five-story building totaled $15,000, and they spent an additional $50,000 on brewing equipment.

A charter was filed in April 1934 for the Dallas Brewery Incorporated, a new and separate enterprise from the pre-Prohibition company of the same name, with capital stock of $70,000. Leiter and Kruse were the only two incorporators, with positions listed as president and secretary-treasurer, respectively. By the time the brewery opened in October 1934, the total amount invested was close to $100,000. Two months later, they announced a $50,000 expansion program along with the election of Lee J. Otto as vice-president and chairman of the board. The money was to go to additional equipment to boost production, enabling the brewery to extend its distribution area around the city.

The brewery's flagship was White Rose Beer, reviving a brand name from the old Dallas Brewery on Houston Street. There was also White Rose Bock Beer, either of which could be found in 1935 grocery store listings, selling at $1.85 for a case of twenty-four bottles. In two years, White Rose cost the same as crosstown rival Schepps at $1.50 per case. National brands like Old Milwaukee, Blatz and Falstaff were no more than twenty-five cents higher, but not one of them approached the $2.60 price tag of Budweiser.

White Rose was also the beneficiary of product placement in a 1937 Sunday feature of the *Dallas Morning News* called "The Model Kitchen and Home." Weekly contests awarded cash prizes for recipes using the ingredients pictured. Dishes included a German-style White Rose Beer Soup, Beef Kidney with White Rose Beer, White Rose Beer Chocolate Cake and these White Rose Toasted Cheese Snacks: "Eight tablespoons prepared mustard. 4 slices white bread. 1 cup White Rose Beer. ½ pound American cheese. 4 slices bacon. Spread bread slices thickly with mustard; lay on a baking sheet and brown lightly in oven. Take out baking sheet; sprinkle bread slices with beer until all is used; cover with slices of cheese ¼ inch thick; lay two half slices of bacon on each. Return to oven and cook until cheese is melted and bacon done. Serve with White Rose Beer."

In May 1936, the Dallas Brewery was operating around the clock and producing over three thousand cases daily. Leiter announced plans to install new machinery and hire more employees to further boost production. The continued expenditures belied what an appeals court judge called the "unsatisfactory condition of the brewery's finances." By May 1943, the Court of Civil Appeals of Texas was considering arguments related to a March 1942 district court ruling against the officers of the brewery.

A summary of the brewery's financial condition showed it was taking notes to avoid overdrafts of its account as far back as 1934. These occurred sporadically through 1935 and 1936 but had become more regular in 1937. In October of that year, a final note to secure $15,000 was issued to the brewery by the Republic National Company. It moved to collect ninety days after issuance, leading to the trial where the only question left to answer was who among the stockholders would foot the bill. Now bankrupt, Dallas

Brewery went into receivership, and assets worth over $125,000 were put up for auction in February 1939.

A FORMER INSURANCE EXECUTIVE, E.F. Anderson, took over the day-to-day operation of the Schepps Brewery at 1026 Young Street after George Schepps resigned as president in March 1939. The following June, the company filed a charter to change its name to Time Brewing Incorporated with the Schepps family maintaining majority ownership. During the transition, a new refrigeration system was installed along with separate chemical and biological laboratories for product testing. Changes also included a new brewmaster and a newly formulated beer.

Time Beer, as it was called, was a lager advertised as "the triumphant achievement in the long and distinguished career of our famous brewmaster." Whether he was famous or not, Rudolph August Bender was certainly well traveled. Born in Germany, Bender started his career as a machinist at the Lone Star Brewing Company of San Antonio. In 1911, he graduated from the Wahl-Henius Institute of Fermentology of Chicago before going on to do postgraduate work at the Hantke Brewers School of Milwaukee, Wisconsin. His return to Texas came after working for breweries in at least five other states. All together, he had over thirty years experience in the brewing industry.

You could try Bender's creation during late-afternoon tours on weekdays at Time Brewing. Guides were on duty daily, ready to show visitors through the brewery and on to the sample room. If the beer was to their liking, Time Beer was fairly inexpensive at a nickel a bottle or $1.19 for a case in May 1941 and also available in twelve-ounce, cone-top cans. Presumably the first canned beer to be offered by a North Texas brewery, a set of three cans was selling for twenty-nine cents in 1940, and in August 1941, the price had dropped to seven and a half cents per can. They may have been trying to sell leftover stock, as by then, the brewery had been sold to a pair of St. Louis businessmen.

9
NORTH TEXAS DURING THE WAR YEARS (1941–1951)

"Hello, Dallas" was the greeting at the top of the ad on the first day Bluebonnet Extra Pale Beer was available for sale in the city. The Dallas–Fort Worth Brewing Company was extending an "invitation to a new, delightful and satisfying experience." It was also meant to be a dare. The person who crafted the message admitted that the marketing-speak would mean nothing if consumers did not like the beer. "Try it and see" was what they were saying in not so many words. "We stake our reputation on your first taste. If we win, you win too." This was how the third brewery to occupy the space at 1026 Young Street in Dallas introduced itself to the city. A large advertising campaign was planned right from the start, and a key selling point was its status as the only North Texas brewery when it opened in June 1941.

Joseph Heutel and Harold W. Mesberg would partner and run the company, with Heutel acting as president and Mesberg as vice-president. Mesberg would also be in charge of sales and marketing, drawing on past experience handling brewery accounts while running his own advertising firm in Milwaukee. Part of his strategy involved cross-promotion with local radio stations. The schedule for a twice-daily program appeared off to the side of their opening-day listing, and the brewery eventually became the name sponsor for two long-running weekly programs called *Bluebonnet Inn* and *Bluebonnet Sports Review*.

As for the beer itself, the idea was to name it after the state flower of Texas and, as the brewery's name implied, release it in both Dallas and

Fort Worth. Bluebonnet Beer would be based on a formula passed down by brewers over three generations and would be billed initially as "one great beer…for two great cities." The company's first brewmaster was Frank Hahn, said to be the grandson of a former brewer at the old Dallas Brewing Company named Paul H. Hahn. He left the brewery after only one year, and his replacement was none other than Rudolph Bender, fresh off a stint at yet another brewery—this time in the state of Iowa.

With Mesberg and Bender on board, sales and technical experience were not in short supply. However, the availability of certain raw materials was another story. The brewery's first four years of existence coincided with the time period during which the United States was actively engaged in World War II. On January 16, 1942, President Franklin D. Roosevelt issued an executive order creating the War Production Board. Its purpose was to oversee the production and allocation of goods needed for the war effort. Items of concern for brewers that fell under the board's purview beyond grain included things like tin, cork and steel.

The first of these to be subjected to restrictions was tin. In February 1942, the board ordered reductions in the manufacture of tin cans and prohibited their use in packaging beer. On the national level, beer packaged in tin cans accounted for 14 percent of sales in the United States. However, it is unclear what effect, if any, this had on the Dallas–Fort Worth Brewery. Tin was used to make bottle crowns, but indications are that smaller brewers were not forced to curtail their usage. On the canning side, Bluebonnet was eventually packaged in cone-tops, which were typically made of steel. If anything, rationing of that material may have been the reason why ads featuring Bluebonnet in that format did not appear until later in the decade. They surely had the capability, considering Time Beer was sold in cans up until the time Heutel and Mesberg took over.

Some items the board regulated actually helped small brewers with competition in their local markets. Curbs on nonessential use of tires and fuel sources meant larger breweries were unable to ship as much product out of state. Although the laws of supply and demand normally dictated an increase in prices, limits set by the General Maximum Price Regulation Act in April 1942 prevented that from happening. Hoping to keep inflation in check and to prevent price gouging during the war, a ceiling was set that did not allow prices to exceed those charged in March of that year. Still, less beer on the shelves from national brands would have given local brewers some level of advantage.

For big producers like Anheuser-Busch, the loss of revenue on interstate sales was probably offset to some degree. They were the ones more likely to be awarded government contracts to supply the troops, thereby increasing their shipments overseas. Large or small, all breweries were required to reserve 15 percent of their production for the armed forces. The combined effort was not enough, leading the government to explore another alternative.

Allan J. Barney, a captain in the United States Army, was one of many involved in an initiative to reconstruct and operate breweries in North Africa and Italy to help meet demand. After the Tunisian campaign in 1943, Barney supervised beer production in the African cities of Casablanca, Oran and Algiers. Later, he moved on to Italy, where he was tasked with retooling Peroni breweries located in Naples, Leghorn and Rome. Following his discharge in 1946, he returned to Anheuser-Busch, the company he had worked for prior to the war in its development and production laboratories. Shortly thereafter, he came to North Texas and was hired by Dallas–Fort Worth Brewing as an assistant brewer in January 1947. Appropriately, an article introducing him noted his impressive list of qualifications and how it brought "additional prestige to the staff."

Other obstacles brewers had to overcome during the war included quotas placed on malted grain. The government wanted to ensure adequate supply levels for companies manufacturing industrial alcohol. This was used in the production of rubber and smokeless gunpowder, both of which were wartime necessities. In September 1943, the Dallas–Fort Worth Brewery was cited for a three-month period between March and May 1943 when it consumed over two and a half times its allotted amount of grain. Heutel told the presiding judge it was used in anticipation of approval on a pending application to increase the brewery's quota. The appeal apparently fell on deaf ears with Heutel pleading guilty and paying a fine of $1,000.

The issue of grain persisted even after the conflict was over. War-torn countries were on the verge of starvation, and President Harry S. Truman called on the American people to carry "their share of the burden." Naturally, wheat and other cereal grains were looked upon as key ingredients in providing food to those in need. In an address given in February 1946, Truman outlined his plan and the measures that needed to be taken. One spoke to brewers directly: "The use of wheat in the direct production of alcohol and beer will be discontinued; the use of other grains for the production of beverage alcohol will be limited…to five days' consumption a month; and the use of other grains for the production of beer will be limited to an aggregate quantity equal to that used for this purpose in 1940 which was 30 percent less than the quantity used in 1945. This will save for food about 20 million bushels of grain."

Estimates on the impact of the restrictions in Texas put the potential number of jobs lost at 3,500, with the state standing to lose $750,000 in tax revenue. Nationally, the amounts totaled 25,000 jobs and over $193 million. Brewers also took issue with the limitations not being extended to grain exports to other countries. They argued places like England, Holland and Mexico would use the grain to make beer and send it back to compete with domestic brewers. Heutel said a further consequence was a loss of federal revenue due to differing tax rates for imports. He gave the example of domestic beer being taxed at $8 a barrel compared to only $7.75 for products from Mexico. Dallas liquor wholesaler and former brewery owner Julius Schepps expressed the feelings of those involved when he said, "The boys abroad should be put on the same level. We should not be penalized because we are Americans."

Except for the ban on wheat for use in alcoholic beverages, most of the curbs from the February order were lifted in November 1946 after a year of good crop yields. Voluntary cutbacks were still encouraged, spurred on partly by the first televised address from the White House in October 1947. In that broadcast, Truman asked the American people to make day-to-day choices in the spirit of food and grain conservation. Brewing industry leaders got together that month and "agreed on a three-month plan to save grain without necessarily causing unemployment or a shortage of beer." Heutel indicated Dallas–Fort Worth Brewing would participate in the program, which called on brewers to reduce corn consumption and not use wheat, table-grade rice or edible barley. The expectation was that brewers would be able to find reasonable substitutes in potatoes and cassava root.

Advertising was something that did not diminish in its use during the war. Dallas–Fort Worth Brewing's near-constant promotional push mirrored a national trend. One estimate had brewers spending $0.96 per barrel on advertising in 1940, an amount that increased to $1.09 by 1950. Like others, while hostilities were still ongoing, the brewery showed its support with ad banners carrying messages like "Back the Attack—Buy U.S. War Bonds" and "Do Your Part in the Seventh War Loan Drive." From there, they evolved from print and radio to take the next step into television. In October 1948, Dallas–Fort Worth Brewing signed a thirteen-week contract with local NBC affiliate WBAP-TV to become the first in the region to sponsor a televised newscast.

An ad in July 1948 claimed Bluebonnet was the top-selling beer in Dallas. However, after the television deal, the brewery's newspaper presence faded. What may have been its final campaign involved the introduction of a new brand called Texas Club in June 1951. Multiple listings, all on the same day in the *Dallas Morning News*, announced its availability. One was nearly a full page, which in addition to boasts like "the greatest treat a thirst for beer can ask," called it "the first and only premium brewed, premium-priced beer…in Texas." Another named the beer as the sponsor of a radio matchmaking program, while still another attributed the recipe to John Delin, an experienced brewmaster whose family brewed the beer for generations. Abruptly, the brewery all but disappeared. In November 1951, assets and fixtures associated with the brewery began appearing daily in the classified section of the newspaper.

THE CLOSING OF THE DALLAS–FORT WORTH BREWING COMPANY meant North Texas was without a brewery for the first time since the repeal of Prohibition. It would stay that way until well into the 1960s. The question of why could be tied to a number of factors. One possibility was demand, something brought up by Henry K. Maas when those behind the pre-Prohibition Dallas Brewery were trying to decide whether to restart the business after repeal. Small brewers depended greatly on regional consumers, but the impact of local-option elections in Texas whittled down the customer base to almost nothing. Portions of Dallas, Tarrant and Palo Pinto Counties in North Texas were wet, but outside of a small concentration in the Panhandle and a few scattered holdouts, nearly every county in the upper half of the state was completely dry as of December 1951.

Another issue was taxation. Beginning in July 1940, the federal government increased the barrel tax three times in eleven years. What was five dollars per barrel when Dallas–Fort Worth Brewing got started jumped to nine dollars by the end of 1951. With each increment, these assessments put the small brewer at a greater and greater disadvantage. Taken together, the effect of all of this meant the days of locally owned and operated breweries were quickly coming to an end, both in Texas and across the country. Smaller operations began to be swallowed up by national and regional producers in the 1940s, starting a trend toward consolidation that would continue for years to come.

10
MILLER BREWING OF FORT WORTH (1963–1990)

The early 1960s saw a statewide boom in brewery construction and expansion—but not on the local level. National brands were stretching across the United States and establishing manufacturing in Texas to serve not only that state's growing consumer base but also the growing population in the Southwest region. By the mid-1960s, new breweries were built in Houston (Anheuser-Busch), Longview (Schlitz) and Fort Worth (Carling) in addition to the existing breweries in Galveston and El Paso (Falstaff), San Antonio (Lone Star, Pearl) and Shiner (Spoetzl).

At this time, Canada's Carling Brewing was the fifth-largest brewery operating in the United States. Looking to expand its North American market, Carling began a long-range plan to put a manufacturing facility in the American Southwest. With the North Texas area quickly developing industrially, enjoying the benefits of a growing interstate highway infrastructure and several national defense contractors building everything from fighter jets to missile controls, the Dallas/Fort Worth area was a natural candidate for the new site.

Even with the expressed desire to build and the promise of jobs and tax revenue, strong opposition was encountered in the form of the familiar conservative and church anti-alcohol groups. Acquiring zoning and permissions for a preferred site in relatively undeveloped south Fort Worth still required a five-year effort and a special act of the Texas legislature to authorize construction of a new brewery in 1961. Although the brewery was to be located in a legally wet area, a special exemption to the state law was required so it could maintain commercial operation should the area ever be rezoned dry in future elections.

"Texas and the Southwest are one of the major growth areas in the United States," said Ian R. Dowie, board chairman for Carling in 1963. The Fort Worth plant was to be Carling's first in the Southwest and its eighth United States facility overall and the first major new brewery constructed in Texas since before World War II. Even though it required a further local-option election to change the status of the specific dry area for the site, it was expected to bring $1 million per year in payroll to the city of Fort Worth.

The new plant was slated to produce Carling's leading national products at the time, its Black Label and Red Cap beers. It was budgeted for $10 million and designed for an overall capacity of 300,000 barrels annually with options for expansion as the American market responded. In anticipation of this new manufacturing site, Carling pioneered an advanced, fully automated "continuous flow process" for brewing and production that was the result of years of dedicated research. This process replaced the traditional batch and kettle brewing method for a web of stainless steel pipes and tanks, all computer-controlled by an operator at a central console. Although fermentation times remained the same, this new process promised a continuous line from raw ingredients to packaged beer. Cutting-edge for its time, the new equipment featured lower costs and less labor and allowed for incremental expansion of the technology as it advanced in the future.

Construction of the new plant began in January 1963 at its location in south Fort Worth, adjacent to the newly constructed Interstate 35W and its junction with Loop 820 (what would soon become the new Interstate 20). The facility attracted national recognition for its forward-looking design and adoption of new construction and manufacturing technologies, and it was named one of the "Top 10" United States manufacturing plants of 1965 as reported by the *Fort Worth Star-Telegram*. Despite being the most advanced brewery in the world at the time, in actual operation, the pioneering "continuous flow process" was plagued with troubles and quickly became a critical liability for the emerging Carling brand.

The Carling plant officially began operation in May 1965 but was shut down "temporarily" in October of that same year, never achieving full production capacity. Sales of its Black Label beer in Texas and the Southwest region were unexpectedly poor (although better in Fort Worth than in any other area), and Carling's overall sales in all fifty states and internationally hit their historic peak in 1964. At the same time, Carling was pressed in a national trademark lawsuit with Philip Morris over the "Black Label" name as well as facing continued local opposition from local Methodist ministers, who publicly called for expulsion of all church members who approved beer sales in local elections.

The Fort Worth facility had planned to create as many as three hundred permanent positions, but Carling never employed more than eighty workers as the "temporary" shutdown inevitably became permanent. Carling's sales had dropped as much as 10 percent across the South and Southwest, and a spokesman referred to the funds spent on the continuous flow brewing technology by commenting that "the Texas problem was a major part of that situation." Although purely a financial failure, local Baptist ministers "prayed for breweries to go broke," and the Baptist General Convention of Texas hailed the closure as "the hand of the Lord" removing the brewery from the proximity of the nearby Southwestern Baptist Theological Seminary in Fort Worth.

WHILE CARLING FOUGHT TO HOLD its place against growing national competition, in 1966 a new investor bought controlling interest in the Miller Brewing Company of Milwaukee, Wisconsin, from the founding Miller family and began a nationwide campaign of expansion. Its first manufacturing facility outside of Wisconsin was acquired in 1966 in Azusa, California, and later that same year, it negotiated to lease but eventually purchased outright the idle Fort Worth plant from Carling as its third national facility.

Miller paid $5.5 million for the existing Carling brewery and would spend the next two and a half years in an extensive overhaul and remodel to the fifty-acre site, abandoning Carling's failed "continuous flow process" technology. It pledged to spend an additional $6 million (later $7.5 million) in upgrades to the location, expanding capacity to 800,000 barrels annually from the original 300,000. New vats and fermentation equipment were brought in as Miller built a five-story brewhouse, doubling the physical size of the old brewery.

With Miller no longer interested in Carling's experimental technology, the used equipment was donated to the J.K. and Susie L. Wadley Research Institute and Blood Bank in Dallas (now Carter BloodCare). The donated items included pumps, centrifuges, filters, stainless-steel vats and various controls, collectively valued at around $1 million, including a thirty-foot electronics instrumentation panel itself worth $100,000. Instead of culturing yeast as intended, Carling's "continuous flow process" for brewing was ideally suited for medical applications, and the gift became the foundation for Wadley's leukemia research with its efficiency in producing the difficult L-asparaginase enzyme for clinical use by the liter.

The new buildings at the Fort Worth location covered 800,000 square feet and would employ as many as 1,125 people, and they included a separate facility adjacent to the brewery for manufacturing aluminum cans and related packaging. By the time Miller began commercial operations in June 1969, the Fort Worth site had become the largest brewery in the state. Its planned output of 800,000 barrels had also been increased to a full 1 million barrels as it began brewing its flagship beer, Miller High Life, and Miller pledged to double that capacity within five years if its current growth continued.

An opening-day ceremony was held at the brewery in September 1969 with a German-themed "*Gemuetlichkeit* Comes to Texas" celebration, complete with German music and specialty foods shipped from Miller's corporate base in Milwaukee. The event was held under a large red-and-white circus tent and attended by six hundred state, county and city officials as well as prominent local business leaders and civic personalities as Miller attempted to embrace its locally adopted city and new regional base of manufacturing for Texas and the Southwest.

On the corporate front, Miller Brewing was bought in 1969 by the multinational Phillip Morris Corporation, which continued to pour money into modernizing and expanding capacity at each of Miller's three United States plants. The Fort Worth location was upgraded to one million barrels by 1971 and to two million barrels by 1975 as increased capacity translated to increased revenue. Still further plans included increasing production to five million barrels and adding six hundred new jobs as part of a $52 million expansion for the Fort Worth site as it supplied beer for Texas and ten other states.

In 1973, Miller permanently shifted the beer world with its newest product, Miller Lite. Test-marketed in four national locations, Miller Lite was the industry's first successful low-calorie ("light") beer, a thin lager boasting only ninety-six calories per twelve-ounce serving, and spurred competitors to develop their own products as the mass-produced light beer era began. The recipe for Miller Lite was not pioneered by Miller itself but acquired through its absorption of smaller New York and Chicago breweries that had already developed their own low-calorie products. Even the trademarked name of "Lite" came from a smaller brewer and was to be the spearhead of numerous national lawsuits as Miller defended its "light" brand name against brewing challengers.

After its official commercial release in January 1975, production of Miller Lite became the primary focus of the brewery in Fort Worth. Consumer response to Miller's product and associated aggressive marketing was tremendous and left Miller dominant in this particular sector. (Miller Lite was so successful its first year that some Texas distributors had to ration supplies to retailers, as the brewery was unable to keep up with full consumer demand.) By 1977, 77 percent of all light-beer sales were Miller Lite, strong enough to pull Miller even with Coors as the fourth-largest brewery in the United States.

By 1983, the Fort Worth Miller plant employed around 1,600 permanent workers, the largest workforce it would ever have at this location. Brands produced at the brewery included Miller Lite, Miller High Life, Löwenbräu and Magnum Malt Liquor. With continued success came continued expansion and upgrades, and the Miller facility in south Fort Worth reached one million square feet by the 1990s.

In June 1990, Miller switched its newest successful product, Miller Genuine Draft, to production at its Fort Worth plant. With another marketing innovation, the production of Genuine Draft differed from other Miller products as it was cold-filtered through a ceramic filter instead of pasteurized and required still further additions and enhancement to on-site equipment for brewing and packaging. Each employee involved in packaging also received an additional two hundred hours of training specifically for the new product.

Now closed, Miller once operated the Miller Marketplace and Brew Kettle Museum as a small-scale historical archive and marketing outlet located adjacent to the working facility in Fort Worth, which served as the base for public relations and the start of factory tours. The dome of the rotunda entrance was made from an actual brewing kettle, and the museum included a history of brewing with particular focus on the Miller corporation and original Frederick Miller family, displaying hundreds of breweriana objects and presentations. Visitors could enjoy samples of Miller products at a museum pub and purchase a variety of branded merchandise in the factory gift store.

The Fort Worth brewery surpassed even its historic Milwaukee plant in 1992, brewing more beer than any other Miller location in the United States as the fully modernized brewery benefited from $24 million in investments to bottle, can and ship more than eight million barrels annually. At that time, Miller Lite was still the best-selling brand of beer in Texas as the Fort Worth brewery reaped the benefits from advances in automation and technology, seeing its full-time personnel numbers drop to just around one thousand employees.

The Fort Worth facility of Miller Brewing continues to operate even today, brewing not only various Miller beers but also contract brewing several lesser brands owned by Miller. Finding a working level at around 625 permanent employees, the facility produces about nine million barrels of beer per year with Miller Lite and Miller Genuine Draft still its primary products. It has become a major contributor to the Tarrant County economy and an integral business and community partner with the city and has found its own place among the brewing culture that is still developing in North Texas.

11
THE BIRTH OF TEXAS MICROBREWING (1982–1990)

Throughout the 1960s and 1970s, the American beer scene became dominated by the national brands and breweries and, to a lesser degree, the emerging import market. Smaller brewers struggled and were eventually absorbed along with their products by these larger international corporations still benefiting from years of outdated regulations at both the state and federal levels. The business of brewing was accustomed to large-scale, national operations and was not prepared for independent businesses on a local, "microbrewing" aspect. Aside from continued success and upgrades to Miller's Fort Worth plant, no other brewing operations existed in the North Texas area for more than a decade.

Lagging behind the rest of the United States by a few years, craft brewing in North Texas began in the early 1980s with a couple of amateurs, Donald and Mary Thompson. They met at the 1973 Oktoberfest in Munich, and after traveling in Europe for a year, they brought their love of local, small-batch beer back to the United States, where they married and decided to make the leap into the brewing business and culture. Don began teaching himself how to homebrew in 1980 and two years later won "Best of Show" at a national competition of the American Homebrewers Association.

Encouraged by their amateur success, the Thompsons decided to take the bold risk of quitting their regular jobs and opened a small package brewery in 1982, the Reinheitsgebot Brewing Company in the Dallas suburb of Plano. *Reinheitsgebot* is the historic German "beer purity law" of 1516 that standardized the brewing ingredients in commercial beers at that time, and the Thompsons intended to focus on traditional Old World beer styles and brewing. Don attended the brewing school at the University of California–Davis, and Mary went to the Siebel Institute of Technology in Chicago as they both tried to absorb all they could about brewing professionally.

Having officially organized and licensed the brewery on paper, it would still be a couple of unexpectedly long years before Reinheitsgebot Brewing made a single drop of beer. They spent those next few years accumulating (or inventing) the specialized equipment necessary to brew beer on such a small scale as well as struggling with suppliers and retailers unaccustomed to dealing with the new "microbreweries" that were unable to handle train-car-full orders of malt.

Don visited California's Sierra Nevada Brewing for professional advice and exposure, and as Mary recalls, "We had no idea it was going to take us three years before we sold our first beer." About two and a half years after legally creating the brewery in a Collin County warehouse, Reinheitsgebot Brewing produced and sold its first beer commercially, Collin County Pure Gold, using Don's same award-winning homebrew recipe. By 1985, the Thompsons had established the first microbrewery not only in Texas but in the greater Southwest region and only the sixth to open in the entire United States.

Reinheitsgebot Brewing eventually produced six hundred barrels a year as it struggled to win over a consuming public still wary of these new "boutique breweries" even with the release of a second beer, a black ale called Collin County Black Gold. The tiny brewery even attracted a visit from famed English beer writer Michael Jackson, who included a mention of Reinheitsgebot Brewing's beers in his 1988 book, *The New World Guide to Beer*. Jackson called the Collin County Pure Gold "an all-malt Pilsener, with a nicely herbal hop character," and the Black Gold "a dry, coffeeish, Munich-style dark beer." Publicity was increasing for the novelty small brewery, but media coverage did not necessarily translate into increased sales.

Reinheitsgebot Brewing closed in 1990 due to inadequate sales revenue and finances after a deal to upgrade its old, used equipment unexpectedly fell through. The Thompsons acknowledged the difficulty in the challenge of their early attempts to change consumers' tastes in commercial beer and to establish a viable brewing business so very different than the industrial brewing giants. "We worked so hard for so long and Texas just wasn't ready," said Mary.

Liquidating their brewing operations, the Thompsons turned their efforts toward working with Davis Tucker on the new laws to legalize brewpubs in the Texas legislature in Austin. Don also briefly found further work as a brewing

Unopened bottles of Collin County Pure Gold and Collin County Black Gold, the first craft beers produced in North Texas by the Reinheitsgebot Brewing Company. *From the collection of Franconia Brewing Company.*

consultant for Dallas Brewing Company, and he and Mary attempted another very short-lived brewpub venture in Dallas just a few years later called Moon Under Water. Don continued to be involved with local Dallas breweries and a few Austin-area brewpubs before eventually finding a position with Tucker at North by Northwest, where he still brews today.

OTHER SMALL BREWERIES BEGAN to open in the years that followed Reinheitsgebot Brewing, encouraged by public exposure to the new national fad of craft beer and microbreweries. The Texas legislature also helped by legalizing the private homebrewing of beer and wine in 1983, which removed some Prohibition-era restrictions for the smaller players in the industry. This act not only allowed private homebrewing activities to flourish but also seeded the market for the commercialization of small-scale, local, craft brewing and a semi-educated brewing workforce and consumer base as they did in many other states.

A second microbrewery, Addison Brewing Company, opened in Addison in May 1988 as the first new brewery to open in Dallas County in nearly fifty years. Brothers-in-law Ken Harbin and Richard House were amateur homebrewers who saw an opportunity with the business-friendly city and, with head brewer John Stuart, sold their first batch of Double-Eagle Amber Lager in November of that same year. A second "dry" beer was put into production soon afterward, but Addison Brewing closed in August 1989 after just one year due to a lack of adequate finances, an unfortunate cycle that businesses would see repeated often with a general public still wary of the new microbrewery movement.

West End Brewing Company opened in March 1989 in the basement of the Brewery, a downtown commercial development recently built in the same warehouse that replaced the historic Dallas Brewing Company of the late nineteenth and early twentieth centuries, producing beer on the site for the first time since 1918. The partners were Allan Dray, a former oilman with no brewing experience, and Jerry Cole, most recently in electronics sales. Dray was drawn to the venture by the new microbrewery movement and invested $500,000 of his own money to create a new brewery in the developing West End Historic District, a downtown Dallas commercial block filled with local shops, restaurants and bars. With an eye toward future franchise opportunities, Dray believed he could somewhat easily change the restrictive Texas alcohol laws to his benefit.

Dray and Cole also established the modern Dallas Brewing Company as a parent company for West End Brewing and as a distributor for Cask Brewing Systems, the Canadian manufacturer of the microbrewery systems used by breweries such as West End Brewing. They planned to brew as many as 5,500 barrels their first year and hired Canadian brewer Gord Slater as their head brewer with Dray focusing on local marketing efforts and selling microbrewery equipment across Texas and the surrounding states. Originally operating as an elaborate malt extract brewer, West End

Like all of the brewery's products, Schepps Xtra Beer was aged in vats of solid redwood. *Courtesy of TavernTrove.com.*

Schepps Xtra Light Lager was an attempt to revive the Schepps family beer brand in 1978. It was brewed at the Spoetzl Brewery in Shiner, Texas. *From the collection of Brian Brown.*

Black Dallas Beer was produced at multiple breweries around the country, including Schepps and Time Brewing, Inc. of Dallas. *Courtesy of TavernTrove.com.*

The first canned beers in Dallas were packaged in cone tops. *Courtesy of BeerCanHistory.com.*

Above: Seasonal beers like the Dallas Brewery's White Rose Bock were made by a number of post-Prohibition breweries in North Texas. *Courtesy of TavernTrove.com.*

Left: John Stuart (upper right) displays his homebrewing awards as the employees of the Addison Brewing Company celebrate their first brew day on November 7, 1988. *From the collection of John Stuart.*

Addison's Double Eagle Lager was modeled after Abita Amber. *From the collection of Brian Brown.*

Other than a change in yeast, Don and Mary Thompson's recipe for Collin County Black Gold is similar to the Okanogan Black Ale served where they currently work at North by Northwest in Austin. County Collin Emerald, a green-colored, all-malt beer brewed in the spirit of Saint Patrick's Day, is a thing of the past. *From the collection of Brian Brown.*

Doing business as the West End Brewing Company, one of the first products out of the Dallas Brewing Company in 1989 was this lager brewed especially for the Outback Pub. *From the collection of Brian Brown.*

Dallas Brewing Company owner Allan Dray referred to Texas Bluebonnet Premium as a "lawnmower beer." It was a pale, light-bodied brew designed to appeal to Coors drinkers. *From the collection of Brian Brown.*

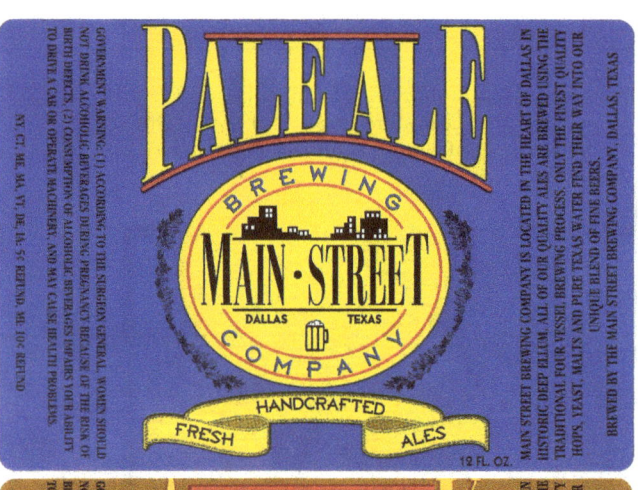

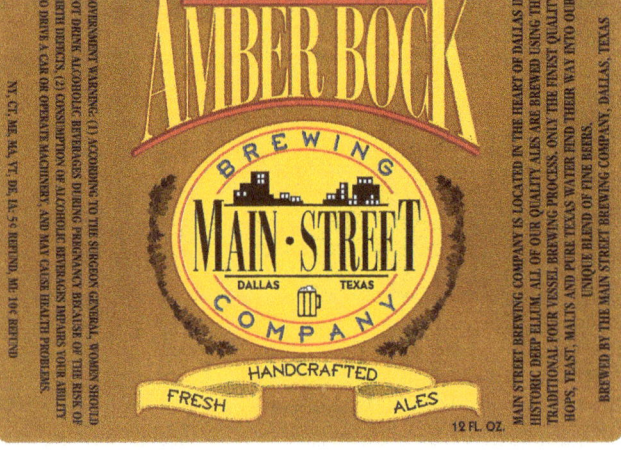

Above: Pint glasses from 1990s-era brewpubs, including one from the first such enterprise in Dallas, the Yegua Creek Brewing Company. In 1994, Yegua Creek joined the Hubcap Brewery and Kitchen as the first brewing operations in the city to win medals at the Great American Beer Festival. *From the collection of Brian Brown.*

Left: Main Street's Pale Ale was a mildly hoppy beer comparable to Bass, while its Amber Bock was described as a smooth, malt-forward brew with no bitter aftertaste. *From the collection of Brian Brown.*

Owner Gary Brown's Routh Street Brewery was praised for its food as well as its crowd-pleasing brews. The restaurant's executive chef, Brian Luscher, went on to become one of the most recognizable names in Dallas's culinary culture. *From the collection of Brian Brown.*

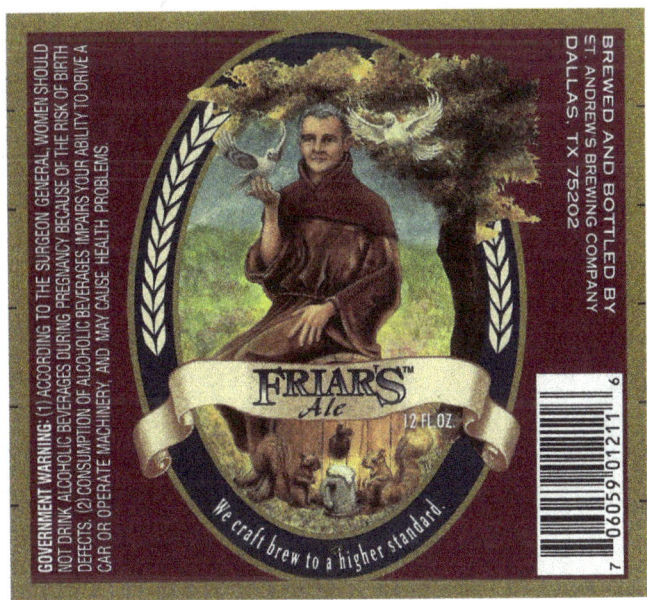

In addition to Friar's Ale, the St. Andrews Brewing Company produced Friar's Light and Friar's Lager. *From the collection of Brian Brown.*

The tap wall at the Deep Ellum Brewing Company features art by the Davies brothers, who are collectively known as Three of One Arts. *Photo by Tait Lifto.*

The theme of the Peticolas Brewing Company's second anniversary celebration was "2 Years 10 Beers." *Photo by Brian Wing.*

Above: Deep Ellum Brewing had a wall of labeled kegs dedicated as a photo area for tour patrons to post their images on social media. *Photo by Paul Hightower.*

Left: Brewers from the five currently operating breweries in North Texas stand together after a locally focused beer dinner hosted by the Common Table on March 5, 2012. *Left to right*: Drew Huerter, Wim Bens, Michael Peticolas, Dennis Wehrmann, Fritz Rahr. *Courtesy of Elliott Snedden Photography.*

Dallas's Four Corners Brewing was an early adopter of cans over bottles and the first in Texas to use the innovative "360 Lid" that removes the entire top of the can. *Photo by Paul Hightower.*

The men behind the beer at the Cedar Creek Brewery in Seven Points. *Left to right*: assistant brewer Blake Morrison, head brewer Damon Lewis and founder Jim Elliott. *Photo by Megan Lewis, Cedar Creek Brewery.*

Community Beer's handmade taps indicate the relative color of their beers. *Photo by Kevin Carr, Community Beer Company.*

Armadillo Ale Works co-founders Bobby Mullins (left) and Yianni Arestis (right) stand among the tanks of their temporary home at the Deep Ellum Brewing Company. *Photo by Gary Payne, University of North Texas.*

Armadillo brews Quakertown Stout to commemorate an African American community that existed inside the city of Denton between 1870 and 1922. *Photo by Andi Harman, Swash Labs.*

The products of Fort Worth's Martin House Brewing Company display the slogan "Made in Texas by Texans." Here they lay in a field of bluebonnets, the state flower of Texas. *Photo by Asa Yoakam, Martin House Brewing Company.*

Above: From the beginning, the founders of Independent Ale Works indicated a preference for malt-forward brews, something evident in the brewery's flagship, a lightly hopped beer called Amber 3.0. *Photo by Chris Graves.*

Left: The Cobra Brewing Company's portfolio includes thematic brews like Anti-Venom Amber Ale and Junior's Snake Bite Jalapeno Pale Ale. *Photo by Chris Graves.*

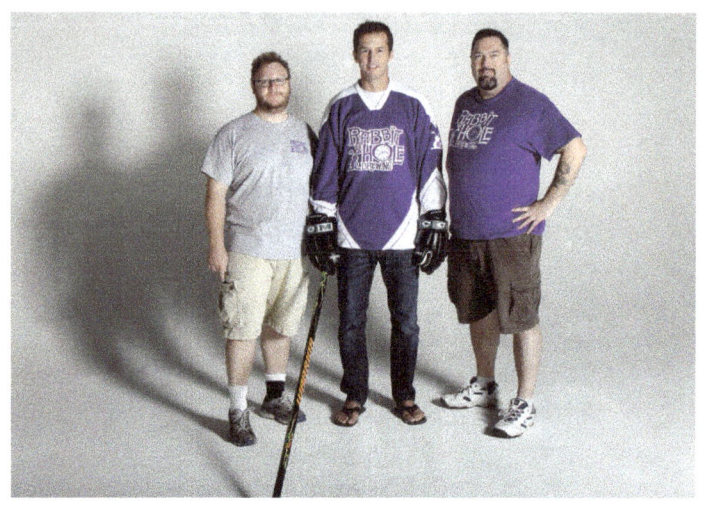

Rabbit Hole Brewing co-owner and brewer Tom Anderson (left) and co-owner Laron Cheek (right) stand beside investor and inspiration, Dallas Stars hockey legend Mike Modano. Rabbit Hole's first beer was named Mike Modano's 561 after his record number of career goals. *Photo by Brian Schoolcraft.*

Dallas Brewing Company founder Allan Dray declared Texas Cowboy to be his favorite among the brewery's offerings. This "full-bodied, bright amber" brew was reported to have "malty aromas and rich, full flavor." *From the collection of Brian Brown.*

Top: Brewed with Australian hops, Outback Lager was the only beer in the Dallas Brewing Company portfolio that was made with hops from outside Washington State. *From the collection of Brian Brown.*

Left: Main Street Brown Ale was a malty, easy-drinking, brown ale similar to Newcastle. The brewery's Raspberry Wheat was created with a mix of black and red raspberries from Oregon to give it a "nice berry aroma without an overpowering taste." *From the collection of Brian Brown.*

Jamie Fulton first entered the North Texas market as the owner of The Covey Restaurant and Brewery in Fort Worth. *Photos by Michael Hiller.*

Left: A break during construction at the Addison Brewing Company. *From the collection of John Stuart.*

Below: Equipment used at Addison Brewing was purchased from the defunct Arkansas Brewing Company. *From the collection of John Stuart.*

Brewing made the switch to all-grain for its commercial beers by August 1991 (which greatly improved the quality of its product), and its first beers were sold on the centennial anniversary of the opening of the original Dallas Brewing Company.

Dray saw a business opportunity in the up-and-coming brewpub trend, a different business model that allowed sales of beer directly to the public. The alcohol laws in most states at this time were based on a strict hierarchy known as the three-tier system: brewers sold to distributors, distributors sold to retailers and retailers sold to the public, with none of the parties allowed to shortcut this model or sell directly to the ultimate consumer. However, brewpubs were prohibited under Texas law, as they did not conform to this three-tier system, and Dray's ownership in a production brewery only further complicated his own legal matters.

As a political vehicle, Dray created and served as executive director of the Texas Association of Small Brewers (also known as the Texas Association of Brewpubs and Microbreweries) in 1990 to lobby for changes to Texas's restrictions on brewpubs and direct-to-consumer distribution. After years of these initial efforts failed, Texas legalized brewpubs in 1993, but restrictions still frustrated Dray in his pursuit of a statewide chain of brewpubs as he was prohibited from owning both types of businesses. Dray actually incorporated his brewing operations under four names—Dallas, Austin, Houston and San Antonio Brewing Companies—with unfulfilled plans for investing up to $2 million in brewpubs across the Lone Star State. He even purchased a ten-thousand-square-foot space on Austin's Sixth Street with the intent of operating a brewpub in that town.

By 1993, Dallas Brewing was renamed the Texas Brewing Company as Dray brought on Don and Mary Thompson from the closed Reinheitsgebot Brewing as partners, hoping to add their brewing experience to his financial management. The Thompsons stayed with Texas Brewing for only a short time, finding Dray difficult to work with personally, before moving on to their own local venture once brewpubs were legalized. Texas Brewing was still the only production brewery operating in Dallas as late as 1995 and the lone North Texas entrant to the Texas Brewers Festival held at the West End Marketplace in April of that year.

Texas Brewing had difficulty selling its beer and even selling the new idea of craft beer. Texans "don't have any couth when it comes to drinking beer," Dray vented at one point to the *Dallas Morning News*. "They want watery beer." However, some contemporary accounts claim that Texas Brewing's product quality was what hurt business as much as difficult management or a disinterested public. Sales continued to struggle until Dray was forced to sell the Texas Brewing name and brand to investors in 1998. The new owners attempted to revive the Texas Brewing label by having it contract brewed at Stroh Brewing in Longview, but the new attempt failed once again after only a year.

ANOTHER DALLAS-BASED BUSINESS, the Richland Beverage Corporation, was started in 1981 by Manny Zelzer to produce a non-alcoholic beer called Texas Select. With an alcohol content of less than 0.5 percent ABV, Texas Select was classified as "alcohol-free" and thus avoided much of the state's regulations as it grew in popularity as the oldest non-alcoholic beer in the United States. Eventually evolving into Texas Select Beverage Company, this near-beer product was contract brewed through Pearl Brewing in San Antonio, with the company still owned and led by Zelzer family members today.

Although these initial attempts at package microbreweries failed, the groundwork and interest had begun to take root in the Dallas area as it did around the state and across the country. Always on the lookout for new business opportunities and now with a small workforce with some brewing experience, the idea of microbreweries as a viable consumer business began to gain favor in North Texas. However, it was the legalization of brewpubs in Texas—one of the last eight states in the United States to do so—that truly lit the flame on the continued interest in craft brewing for Dallas and the surrounding cities.

12
TEXAS LEGALIZES BREWPUBS
(1993–2001)

In August 1993, after four legislative sessions of grass-roots lobbying efforts by small brewers, Texas became the forty-second state to legalize and license the commercial brewpub (HB 1425). The law went into effect on September 1 with strict guidelines to satisfy the opponents of the bill—mostly wholesale distributors—that capped production and regulated brewpubs to on-premise sales only. (Technically, brewpubs were not recognized as full breweries but as simple retailers, still unable to enter the beer distribution channels.) At passing, three brewpubs were already in the planning stages in Dallas and Austin, and the new law would spawn the opening of dozens more in the following years.

Yegua Creek Brewing Company (pronounced *YAY-wah*, named after a Central Texas river) opened in January 1994 as Dallas's first and Texas's second commercially licensed brewpub. Owner and veteran Dallas restaurateur Toby O'Brien opened his 9,200-square-foot brewpub in a historic icehouse on North Henderson Avenue off Central Expressway. Brewer Rob Cromie produced about 1,400 gallons of beer each week and initially suffered in quality from its own popularity as beers were often served before being allowed to fully carbonate. The kitchen became known for incorporating its beer into its "Tex-ethnic menu" such as stout-battered fried mushrooms and featuring exotic, gourmet dishes like smoked venison, boar sausage, rabbit and pizza topped with emu or pheasant.

Following quickly on the heels of Yegua Creek was Hubcap Brewery and Kitchen, opening in an eight-thousand-square-foot space on North Market Street in Dallas's West End in June 1994. This brewpub was a spin-off venture of a Vail, Colorado original concept owned by Dean Liotta and a couple of Texas partners, Jim Poynter and Kelly Jones. Brewers Patrick Carroll and Mike Kraft left jobs in engineering for brew training at Chicago's Siebel Institute of Technology to work in Hubcap's brewhouse, which benefited greatly from its downtown positioning.

Two Hoffbrau Steaks and Brewery stores opened as brewpubs in 1995, one on Belt Line in Addison (February) and one on Knox Street in Dallas (September). Instead of being a new brewpub concept, Hoffbrau Steaks was a local restaurant chain with several locations operating around North Texas since 1978 and decided to retrofit dining areas as in-house brewing operations. The steakhouse-as-brewpub concept employed Steven Sandidge, a former employee of Miller Brewing in Fort Worth, as its head brewer along with senior brewers Johnny Morrison and Tim Deemer. With Morrison at the Addison location and Deemer working in Dallas, the Addison Hoffbrau won a silver medal at the Great American Beer Festival (GABF) in 1995 for its Yellow Rose Cream Ale, merely a month after opening.

With the business model now legalized in Texas, out-of-state brewpub franchises began to eye the state as a potential expansion market. Colorado-based brewpub chain Rock Bottom Brewing opened a North Texas location in Addison in May 1995. This brewpub was the sixth in the national chain headquartered out of Boulder and the second already in Texas (after Houston) and employed John Oliphant as a brewer. With color photographs of Colorado lining the walls, the brewpub offered an aspiring nationally standard food menu that tried, like many others, to offer dishes a level above simple pub grub.

An Oklahoma-based concept associated with the Tulsa Brewing Company, TwoRows Restaurant and Brewery, opened in Greenville Avenue's Old Town Shopping Center in Dallas in May 1995, the third location for the brewpub chain after Oklahoma and Houston. The business owners were Kenny Tolbert, Robert Ross, Rusty Loeffler and Mike Brotzman, with Brotzman serving as the original brewer for the Dallas location. Later brewers included Mike Kraft, who won a bronze medal at the GABF in 2000.

The Routh Street Brewery and Grille opened in September 1995 in the Uptown area of Dallas off Cedar Springs. Owner Gary Brown offered a smaller, cozier pub feel than the Yegua Creek or Hubcap brewpubs with a more traditional Texas menu and a decor reminiscent of the Hill Country;

The original Humperdinks location on Greenville Avenue in Dallas was converted to a brewpub in 1997. *Photo by Brian Brown.*

the local *Dallas Observer* reviewer at the time ranked it as "the best brewpub to date" in Dallas. Routh Street's brewer was Al Kinchen, an accomplished homebrewer and nationally ranked beer judge, but the beers produced were described as plain crowd-pleasers with a "tendency to aim for the big fat middle of the road."

Another out-of-state brewpub chain, Big Horn Brewing from the Pacific Northwest, ventured into Texas beginning in the mid-1990s with its parent company, Ram International, operating as a more local endeavor named Texas Ram Corp. Texas restaurateur John McMurray opened his original Humperdinks sports bar on Greenville Avenue in Dallas in 1976 and decided to expand by partnering with the Washington-based Big Horn Brewing as Humperdinks Restaurant and Brewery, beginning with a Richardson location in 1991. Building on his very successful, over-the-top sports bar concept—one of the first to provide events via satellite—McMurray used the addition of in-house brewing to provide a proprietary product that was cheaper than commercial brands and breathed new life into his aging business concept. He eventually established his model of local brewpub by making corporate-standard recipes at each of its multiple Metroplex locations with head brewer Thomas Janik, who stayed with Humperdinks for the next seventeen years.

A new Humperdinks location opened in Arlington in 1995 just down the road from Six Flags Over Texas, the first brewpub to open in Tarrant County and billed as the "Tallest Bar in Texas" with its towering two-story backdrop behind the bar. The original Greenville Avenue location reopened with brewing operations after a remodel in 1997. Eventually, a total of seven North Texas Humperdinks were to follow, including one in Irving (Las Colinas), a second in Dallas on Northwest Highway in 1997 and one in Addison in 1998. The Addison location was officially certified as the "World's Tallest Bar" by the *Guinness Book of World Records* and took home a silver medal at the GABF the same year it opened. (The Irving location was also the site of a tragic murder-suicide in 1996 as a distraught lunchtime customer shot his girlfriend and the Humperdinks day manager before turning the gun on himself.)

TEXAS WAS NOT WITHOUT its own franchised brewpub ventures. Austin-based Copper Tank Brewing Company opened its second location in the Deep Ellum entertainment district of Dallas's Main Street in January 1996. It occupied a cavernous space at Main and Good-Latimer, with a separate entrance on Commerce Street and a warehouse feel and decor secondary to the exposed metal tanks. Owners Aaron Sharff and Mark Francois hired brewers Rob Cartwright and Patrick Carroll, who won two medals at the GABF in 1998. Unlike other Dallas brewpubs, Copper Tank was praised for its beer by reviews such as the *Dallas Observer* stating, "Unlike many of the anemic beers concocted in brew pubs, each of these was full-flavored and distinct." At one point it claimed to have the "No. 1 selling brew-pub beer in Texas," its Copper Light. Over the years, it was fairly successful and employed several North Texas brewers, including John Sims, who won a gold medal at the GABF in 2000.

Panther City Brewery and Café, Fort Worth's first independent brewpub named for that town's historic nickname, opened in March 1996 in the Stockyards National Historic District north of downtown. General manager Darryl Ireland took Panther City beers to the Texas Brewers Festival held at Sundance Square for the first time that fall, taking advantage of the law change the previous year allowing brewpubs to sell their beers outside pub property. The Austin-based festival held annual events remotely in Dallas, Fort Worth, Houston and San Antonio in addition to its primary celebration in downtown Austin. In 1996, it drew a number of local brewpub entries at each location because of the recently amended state law. Ultimately, Panther City proved a marketing mismatch, offering a contemporary southwestern decor and menu against the heavy-western cowboy motif of the Stockyards historic district. It closed before the end of its first calendar year of operation.

In August 1996, Dallas's Moon Under Water opened in an expansive space in Deep Ellum, mere blocks away from Copper Tank Brewing. The new brewpub occupied an old warehouse dating back to 1910, composed of four different buildings and large enough to have two addresses, one on Main Street and one on Elm. Named for a George Orwell literary reference, Moon Under Water was a subsequent venture of Don and Mary Thompson, formerly of Reinheitsgebot Brewing and Texas Brewing, partnering with restaurateur Steve Hughes and his wife, Julie, as their first attempt at a brewpub business.

Moon Under Water was conceived as more of a jazz and live music venue than a traditional brewpub, a "restaurant and rhythm room" as it was billed. It was divided between two larger rooms, the Main Street side open and spacious with brewing tanks on display and the Elm Street side smaller and more intimate with white-tablecloth dining. The exposed brick walls framed a large floor-to-ceiling, moon-themed mural in the larger room in front of a space for bands to play after hours, and the club included six hundred square feet of dressing rooms, offices and showers in a plan to attract national acts. Space was provided for dancing, and even a small gift shop was available to sell brewpub-branded merchandise.

Despite making good beers, Moon Under Water had trouble with its food (a "Mediterranean menu with Southwestern influences" that changed after the original chef was fired) and was panned by critics in both the *Dallas Morning News* and the *Dallas Observer*. With a long-standing personal rift between the Hugheses and the Thompsons over money, debt and management, the brewpub closed in November due to "undercapitalization" and a host of legal and financial problems after only two months of disappointing operation. Its equipment was eventually sold to Copper Tank Brewing founder Davis Tucker as he and Don Thompson turned their attention to Austin and established the North by Northwest brewpub on the north side of town, where Thompson served as head brewer.

Texas also had its share of instant brewpub flops. The Fort Worth Brewing Company was scheduled to open in 1994 (but never did) in Sundance Square's Land Title Building, the historic structure that would house the original Flying Saucer Draught Emporium a year later. A Dallas copy of Breckinridge Brewery opened as a brewpub in May 1996 with an open brewhouse design and decorations that relied heavily on the winter skiing and related activities of its Colorado namesake. With Jeff Williams as its head brewer, Breckinridge experienced technical problems with its brewhouse and had to supply beer from its Denver brewery and closed before it saw a full year of operations, never having brewed a drop on site. Sir William's Restaurant and Brewery was planned to open near the new Grapevine Mills mall when that development opened in 1997, but the brewpub never progressed past the development stages.

EVEN AMONG THE NEW BREWPUB POPULARITY, traditional package microbreweries continued to open. Joe Contreras and Jim Wisniewski took over the lease for the building that once housed the new Dallas Brewing Company and established the St. Andrews Brewing Company in 1994. Contreras was a chef and biochemist, and Wisniewski was a former employee of Anheuser-Busch. St. Andrews began brewing and bottling beers under the "Original Friar's" label, a reference to their company's sixth-century Roman namesake.

February 1996 saw a new production brewery, the Main Street Brewing Company, open in Deep Ellum, with co-owners George Corey and Greg Correard and former Yegua Creek brewer Rob Cromie. Correard brought brewing experience from H.C. Berger Brewing of Colorado, and George Corey had a background in radio marketing. After only a few months, Main Street was ahead of its initial projections and successful enough to sign with a Miller distributor. Neither St. Andrews nor Main Street Brewing lasted more than a couple of years before closing.

In the midst of craft breweries and brewpubs, a new concept in beer bars was developed in downtown Fort Worth. The Flying Saucer Draught Emporium opened in the historic Land Title Building in 1995, a megabar specializing in more than seventy taps on a brass draught wall and a beer menu that spanned four pages. The Flying Saucer was created by local developer Shannon Wynne, who was inspired by the similar model adopted by the Dallas location of the Ginger Man that opened in 1992. Whereas the Ginger Man maintained a traditional English pub feel, the Flying Saucer was more modern with an expanded waitstaff and food menu and quickly took the reins for promoting craft beer and related local events. A loyalty program called the UFO Club allowed members to track the beers they drank and awarded them a plate on the wall when they accumulated two hundred different beers. With its sister club 8.0 (both owned by Wynne's group of developers), the Flying Saucer became the cornerstone for the Sundance Square entertainment district in downtown Fort Worth. The Flying Saucer concept proved enormously successful and popular, with locations eventually opening in Arlington, Dallas, Addison, Garland and throughout Texas and other southern states.

A Full-Bodied History of Brewing in Dallas, Fort Worth and Beyond

The Dallas Brewery Building is built on the site of the pre-Prohibition Dallas Brewing Company. It was also home to the modern-day Dallas Brewing Company and the St. Andrews Brewing Company in the 1990s. *Photo by Brian Brown.*

Despite the perceived enthusiasm for the new brewpub businesses, the public tastes were hard to win over to locally made craft beer. In 1997, the Addison and Houston locations of Rock Bottom were listed as their worst performers of the fourteen stores operating nationwide at that time. Even with overall growth across the country, the North Texas location of this brewpub chain attempted to compete by brewing Dallas Light (only available in Texas) and was forced to add the major commercial bottled brands to its menu to satisfy local customers.

In Fort Worth, the USA Café (USA Brewing Company) opened downtown in March 1997 in a twenty-two-thousand-square-foot space on Commerce Street opposite Sundance Square and facing the original, one-year-old Flying Saucer. This location was a test-market concept pioneered by Dallas nightclub developer Lance McFaddin for a projected national brewpub chain to compete with Planet Hollywood. Featuring a patriotic Americana theme, its front façade included an oversized Statue of Liberty and brightly lit American flag jutting out over an entrance that included panoramic mock-ups of Mount Rushmore. Steven Sandidge, formerly of Hoffbrau Steaks, was the original head brewer, and the below-street-level restaurant location included a six-thousand-square-foot brewpub that won two gold medals at GABF in 1997.

Bar area of the Flying Saucer Draught Emporium in its original location in Fort Worth's Sundance Square. Members of the UFO Club gain customized plates on the wall for beer-drinking milestones. *Photo by Paul Hightower.*

Left: The USA Café, which opened in Fort Worth's Sundance Square in 1997, was a theme restaurant intended to be in the same market niche as Planet Hollywood and the Hard Rock Café. *Courtesy of TimJohnsonCreative.com.*

Below: In line with its patriotic theme, the tanks in the brewhouse of the USA Café were named after former United States presidents. *Courtesy of TimJohnsonCreative.com.*

Despite its brief success and ultimate failure, the fate of the USA Café brewpub must be considered with a grain of salt compared to other local brewpub closures. Although it did enjoy some local popularity, the USA Café was never intended to be a permanent business as it almost continuously evolved from its initial concept after opening, refining and testing various business models. It abandoned brewing operations just one year after opening, installed a dance floor and toyed with an upscale remodel as the Great American Steakhouse before closing for good in late 1998.

Great Grains Brewery opened as a package brewery in Dallas in March 1997 with homebrewers and Texas Tech classmates Joe Cheatum and Alex Pastrana as owners. In addition to its own brewing efforts, Great Grains achieved some level of ongoing success by purchasing the brands of other Texas microbreweries as those efforts closed, such as Hill Country Brewing and Yellow Rose Brewing, and continuing to brew its beers under the original brewer's label. (At one point in 2001, Great Grains produced twelve of the twenty-five total Texas microbrewed beers.) Great Grains also leveraged more revenue by distributing in Texas for a small number of out-of-state breweries such as New York's Brewery Ommegang and Colorado's Great Divide Brewing.

THE DOWNWARD SLIDE FOR DALLAS BREWPUBS began in the late 1990s with a combination of market oversaturation and simply an abundance of poor quality beers, and the trend continued for several more years with very little positive news for the Dallas area. In mid-1997, a publicly held venture called Schooner Brewery acquired the foundering Hubcap Brewery and in September contracted with Connect Computer Solutions in Euless to develop an interactive video-gaming system for use in its brewpubs. Despite winning a silver medal at the 1998 World Beer Cup, in January 1999, Schooner Brewery changed its name to GameCon, Inc. and shifted its focus solely to online gaming. The parent company closed both the Dallas Hubcap Brewery and its Colorado predecessor in March of that same year.

Yegua Creek closed in September 1998, in large part due to the nearby construction of the new Central Expressway (U.S. Highway 75). Located just a block away from the new highway, roadwork restricted traffic and access to local businesses, and sales at the brewpub were cut almost in half since the highway expansion began in 1995. Owner Toby O'Brien attempted to negotiate a new space and relocate along McKinney Avenue in the Uptown area of Dallas, but Yegua Creek never reopened. After five years of merely break-even revenue, the owners of Routh Street Brewery and Grille made a business decision to abandon their on-premise brewing operations and proceed as a restaurant only in April 2000. The Hoffbrau Steaks chain was sold off to new ownership in 2001, ending its local brewpub operations when both Addison and Dallas locations closed in October of that year. The Dallas Copper Tank location in Deep Ellum was also abandoned in October 2001 because of decreasing revenue.

Although this business purge would leave Dallas without any independent brewpubs, sparks of life could still be seen occasionally in the North Texas microbrewing industry around the turn of the twenty-first century. The expansive Grapevine Mills Mall opened in 1997 as the largest mall in Tarrant County, and with it came major upgrades to adjacent highways as well as attracting surrounding stores, a hotel and even a resort to the same vicinity. The sporting and outdoor retailer Bass Pro Outdoor World opened a flagship store in the area and wanted an accompanying restaurant concept with this new Grapevine location. Instead of a local start-up, Bass Pro enticed a Michigan-based brewpub chain, Big Buck Brewery and Steakhouse, to open a hunting lodge–themed location in a cathedral-like connected space in August 2000, the only location outside Michigan.

In April 2000, Steven Sandidge (formerly of Hoffbrau Steaks and USA Café) and Gary Lopez started the Texas Beer Company in Fort Worth, taking over a small 7-Up bottling facility located just north of downtown on the Paddock Viaduct across the Trinity River. Even with its relatively late appearance on the North Texas brewing scene, Texas Beer Company was the first package microbrewery to open in Fort Worth. Sandidge and Lopez met while employed at Fort Worth's Miller Brewing, and their brewery's flagship product, Texas Light, was designed to compete in the local market against the national low-calorie, light lager brands. The brewery closed in December 2001 as a result of poor financial backing available in the downturn following the September 11th World Trade Center attacks.

In 2003, Dallas's Great Grains Brewing leased the spot formerly occupied by Texas Beer Company, looking to expand its capacity by relocating to the new 7,500-square-foot facility in Fort Worth. Moving its brewing operations in May 2004, Great Grains was abruptly shut down by the Texas Alcohol Beverage Commission (TABC) because of a technicality: the labels used for its bottled products still listed its Dallas address instead of its new Fort Worth facility, as well as reusing old labels of the now-defunct breweries whose products it bought and continued to brew. Previously assured by regulators that the former labels would still be adequate, Great Grains was left without funds for reprinting all labels to comply with regulations and was forced to close. Its brewhouse equipment was eventually sold to a Danish microbrewery the following year.

The loss of Great Grains was not particularly a tragedy for the North Texas brewing industry despite another brewery closing. Great Grains long suffered from quality issues and poor brewing practices and often overextended its business focus beyond craft beer to contract-brew custom "malt beverages" for local organizations. Contamination became common in its bottled beers as the brewery failed to manage its distributed products, which would sit on retailer shelves for years. One local claim to infamy was an original brown ale called Texas Tornado, which began well, but popular consensus would eventually herald toward the end of the Great Grains operation as the worst craft beer ever produced in Texas.

California-based BJ's Restaurant and Brewhouse opened its first Texas location in 2003 in Lewisville and, beginning in 2007, proceeded to open locations across the state in each of the major metropolitan areas as part of its national eastward expansion. BJ's traditional model of shared, distributed brewing was prohibited under Texas alcohol statutes (the state would require each brewpub to be licensed independently), but the brewpub chain reached an agreement with Houston's Saint Arnold Brewing to contract-brew its own recipes for all of their Texas stores. Today, new BJ's Restaurant and Brewhouses are still opening in Texas and thriving with nine locations in the Greater North Texas area.

The remnants of the 1990s brewpub efforts lingered for years in North Texas into the new millennium, with no new opportunities for more than a decade. TwoRows opened a new brewpub location in Addison in 2003 on the Dallas North Tollway in an effort to reboot the franchise, which only lasted until 2009. Its last Greenville Avenue location remained open and brewing until the summer of 2008, all closing for financial reasons. A local TwoRows Classic Grill still remains open today in Allen, but this location never had in-house brewing operations.

While forced to close all but four of its Humperdinks brewpubs for similar declines in revenue, in 2006, these North Texas brewpubs were bought out from their parent company, Big Horn Brewing, and reorganized under the corporate name Humperdinks of Texas as an in-state, local company. With North Texas ownership and direction once again, they consolidated their on-site brewing efforts to just a few of their brewpubs in Dallas, Addison and Arlington, where they remain open and thriving even today.

13
REBUILDING FOR TODAY'S CRAFT BEER (2004–2010)

With the Deep Ellum location of Copper Tank Brewing packing up in 2001, new brewing ventures in North Texas abandoned Dallas for the next decade. Even with a relatively strong regional economy and established beer-bar chains like the Flying Saucer, Ginger Man, Fox and Hound English Pub and a host of independent, Irish-themed pubs, the Dallas market could not sustain its taste for locally produced beer. Instead, the brewing torch was passed to the cities surrounding Dallas County as each found its own microbrewing traditions.

Locally owned brewing returned to North Texas in 2004 by way of Manitowoc, Wisconsin. Frederick "Fritz" Rahr descended from a German brewing family of the Midwest who transitioned from brewing to a very successful malting business during Prohibition and afterward continued to provide grain and feed instead of returning to active brewing operations. Rahr came to the state to attend Texas Christian University (TCU), graduated and settled down to raise a family in his adopted home of Fort Worth. An amateur homebrewer and formally educated in logistics, he found a career with the railroads headquartered in North Texas but continued to dream of returning to his family roots of brewing locally made beers.

Enduring the tedium of a corporate career for years, Fritz eventually decided to make the jump from amateur brewer to professional. After graduating from Chicago's Siebel Institute of Technology as well as study in Germany, he opened the Rahr & Sons Brewing Company in September 2004 in an old Coca-Cola warehouse in the industrial district just south of

Front porch of the Ginger Man, Dallas, the second location of the Texas beer-bar chain and oldest dedicated craft beer bar in the North Texas area. *Photo by Paul Hightower.*

downtown Fort Worth. The brewery maximized its local Cowtown image in labels and advertising as well as playing on the Rahr family name with the marketing tagline, "The brand new beer with a 150-year history." It opened for Saturday tours and tastings almost immediately, as these proved to be its "least expensive form of advertising."

Rahr & Sons' first brewer was the award-winning Jason Courtney, formerly of Hub City in Lubbock, who worked with Fritz to install the brewery and develop the initial recipes. A succession of local Texas brewers followed soon after Courtney departed for his own brewing venture, replaced by James Hudec, Fritz Rahr himself, Gavin Secchi, J.B. Flowers and Jason Lyon. The

Fritz and Erin Rahr represent Rahr & Sons at the Texas Beer Fest in Humble, Texas, on May 7, 2011. *Photo by Ronnie Crocker, Houston Chronicle.*

Rahr & Sons Brewing's eighth anniversary in 2012 was celebrated at the brewery with more than 2,300 attendees enjoying thirty-six different beers, all brewed by Rahr & Sons. *Photo by Paul Hightower.*

original lineup of beers was strongly German-styled after Rahr's family history, but as the brewery grew, non-German and contemporary styles were also added to its portfolio.

For its first few years of operation, Rahr & Sons distributed its own beers and built a strong local brand and following from Fort Worth businesses and consumers. Afternoon tours of the brewery, offered every Saturday since opening, developed a familiar and festival quality as crowds of hundreds—occasionally over one thousand—regularly attended, many becoming weekly fixtures. Particularly popular was Rahr's Ugly Pug Black Lager, named after his mother-in-law's dog, Oscar, and strikingly different for modern craft brewing as one of the first *schwarzbiers* to be brewed and bottled in Texas.

The first few years after opening proved to be a financial strain for this lone brewery operating in North Texas. Rahr & Sons relied heavily on a large contingent of fiercely loyal amateur volunteers willing to work for trade, mostly assisting in bottling and packaging and staffing the Saturday tours. A distribution deal was eventually signed with regional Andrews Distributing in 2005, allowing Rahr & Sons beers to be available over a much wider area outside of Fort Worth.

By 2006, growing financial pressures forced Fritz to lay off most of his employees and take on brewing operations himself. A year later, Fritz took on Tony Formby as an investor and managing partner to keep his brewery operating, providing some needed stability with revenue and continued growth. The investment by Formby allowed Rahr & Sons to moderately expand, hiring Gavin Secchi as brewer in 2007 followed by J.B. Flowers later that same year. The brewery even considered expanding its capacity as demand for its beers continued to slowly rise.

At about that same time, Fritz was offered a very lucrative position working for an oil company based out of the Caribbean. Always an award-winning swimmer and boating enthusiast, Fritz relocated his family to the United States Virgin Islands for a two-and-a-half-year sabbatical from the brewery while maintaining ownership and remote direction. Formby was left to manage much of the daily operations and marketing of Rahr & Sons as Fritz returned to town on a semi-monthly basis to oversee the general direction of his brewery.

Now moderately successful, Rahr & Sons expanded in 2009 to a brewing capacity of six thousand barrels annually as it continued to add to its product line with new beers and new recipes. Its success continued with a number of medals awarded at various national competitions including the Great American Beer Festival, World Beer Cup and United States

A Full-Bodied History of Brewing in Dallas, Fort Worth and Beyond

After packaging its beer in bottles since December 2004, Rahr & Sons introduced its first canned beer in May 2014. Pride of Texas Pale Ale was available exclusively in this format. *Courtesy of Rahr & Sons Brewing Company.*

Service area at the weekly tour at Rahr & Sons Brewing in Fort Worth. Saturday tours can regularly attract crowds of several hundred or even more than one thousand for special events and releases. *Photo by Paul Hightower.*

Brewers Association president Charlie Papazian presents Rahr & Sons with a bronze medal for Stormcloud during the 2014 World Beer Cup. The beer was recognized in the English-Style IPA category. *Photo by Jason E. Kaplan.*

Beer Tasting Championship. Rahr & Sons also continued its community involvement with sponsored charities, homebrewing competitions, minimarathons and even a local soccer team, FC Rahr. Fritz returned to North Texas that summer with enough capital to buy out Formby and resume operating control of his brewery just as demand for his local craft beer was peaking.

The worst damage in Texas brewing to date arrived at Rahr & Sons on a wintry February night in 2010. Awakened in the early morning hours by alarm alerts from his brewery, Fritz arrived to find that the weight of the record snowfall overnight (officially twelve and a half inches in North Texas) had partially collapsed the main roof of the building. As it was overnight, no one was harmed, but the brewery and offices were flooded with a foot of water from burst pipes, and much of the equipment was damaged by water or falling structure. The interior stood exposed to the sky, and in some places, fermentation vessels were all that was supporting pieces of the building. As Fritz so aptly described his brewery at the time,

Record snowfall overnight in February 2010 caused the main roof at Rahr & Sons Brewing to collapse under the weight, shutting down the brewery for months as they rebuilt. *Photo by Jamie Brunner.*

With brewery piping running along the underside of the roof, Rahr & Sons Brewing was flooded with more than a foot of water when its roof collapsed. *Photo by Jamie Brunner.*

Fermentation tanks and other equipment were all that supported the roof in places. *Photo by Jamie Brunner.*

"Someone unzipped my roof." Tours and production were suspended indefinitely until damage could be assessed and the facilities repaired.

Bottled stock was immediately picked up by local Coors Distribution, but the assessment of the brewery's condition left it at least three months out of resuming production. Insurance covered much of the expenses of rebuilding the warehouse structure as well as upgrading the damaged bottling line and a few other pieces of equipment. Taking advantage of the unfortunate spotlight, a series of self-deprecating viral ads produced by Rahr & Sons that depicted the idle brewers trying to occupy their time through the rebuild became popular.

Brewing production was resumed by June of that same year, followed by an opportunity to rebrand its products with a new logo and label design. The event has become commemorated in Rahr & Sons' brewing lineup with the annual release each February of its strong oatmeal stout, Snowmageddon. The roof collapse provided a soft "reboot" for Rahr & Sons, allowing it to embark on a plan of moderate expansion both in staff and brewing ability, most recently hiring Craig Mycoskie as head brewer. With success throughout the Fort Worth and Dallas area, Rahr & Sons has reached a total annual capacity of twenty thousand barrels and continues to grow on all fronts.

NEARLY ON THE OPPOSITE SIDE of the Metroplex from Rahr & Sons, Franconia Brewing opened north of Dallas in McKinney in February 2008. A German national and third-generation brewer, Dennis Wehrmann followed his family's brewing heritage and established his own independent brewing traditions in North Texas with an eye on re-creating authentic German recipes and brewing techniques. A graduate of the Doemens Academy in Munich, he came to the United States in 2003 as head brewer for the TwoRows Restaurant and Brewery location in Addison until 2007. (Franconia contract-brewed the beers for TwoRows until that location closed in the summer of 2009.)

True to his European nature, Wehrmann approached brewing with a very "green" and waste-averse business model. Instead of leasing an existing industrial warehouse like most brewing start-ups, he had a building custom designed and built in a McKinney industrial park. Smaller than most young microbreweries, the state-of-the-art facility was intended to be extremely efficient on many levels, including a low electricity demand in the brutal Texas summers, extensive recycling of used water (up to 85 percent), specially insulated floors and having no dumpster for refuse, with only a single trash can anywhere on the premises. Wehrmann initially hired Gavin Secchi as brewer and later hired Cam Horn, a graduate of the Siebel Institute of Technology, in 2011.

A tragedy was narrowly avoided in February 2012 when pressure accumulated in a fermentation vessel and it burst during one of Franconia's regular Saturday tours. Likely building for hours or days from a blocked pressure valve, the release was powerful enough to send a full fermenter through an interior wall and into the adjacent room, spraying the interior of the brewery with beer. Only minutes prior, Wehrmann had led a tour group of eighty to one hundred guests from the room into the adjacent walk-in cooler, thus avoiding greater casualties. The accident injured two people, neither seriously, and an undisclosed settlement was eventually reached without legal action.

Franconia was slow to adopt a bottling program for its beers, with bottles first appearing on retailer's shelves as late as 2013. Wehrmann was unhappy with domestic bottling practices as he saw them as inefficient and full of wasteful packaging. He initially wanted to use returnable bottles with a

Franconia Brewing Company founder Dennis Wehrmann taps a keg dating back to the early 1800s. Wehrmann has acquired a number of such kegs, all of which were originally used in a brewery owned by his great-great-grandfather Schaubert. *Photo by Suresh Chatlani.*

The image of Wehrmann's great-great-grandfather Schaubert sits atop the label of every Franconia brew. *Photo by Brian Brown.*

Fashioned in the shape of a keg, Franconia's power generator utilizes vegetable oil, solar power and natural gas to supply all of the brewery's energy needs. *Photo by Brian Brown.*

traditional swing-top design but could never establish an adequate or profitable recovery program with local businesses. "Bottling just never fit into our environmental focus," Wehrmann said in an interview with the *Dallas Observer*. "There's no real process for making sure the bottles are recycled or reused."

Bottled beers were a business compromise for Franconia as it was forced to respond to growing market pressure and local competition. However, that decision came only after the installation of a revolutionary new energy

Members of the Franconia crew bring their tankards together after the ceremonial tapping of the keg at the 2013 McKinney Oktoberfest. *Photo by Beth Shumate, McKinney Convention and Visitors Bureau.*

unit for the brewery that was a self-contained hybrid of solar, biofuels and natural gas. As the only brewery in the world to adopt the new "micropower generation" technology, Franconia successfully went off the North Texas electrical grid in 2013 and is today completely energy-independent.

THE ESTABLISHMENT OF RAHR & SONS and Franconia was accompanied by only a single other local production craft brewing operation. Former computer consultant and amateur brewer Ken March developed a microbrewery concept called Healthy Brew in 2003 with a facility located in north Fort Worth. March's dream was to produce quality organic beers, and to that end, he spent a great deal of personal resources attempting to gain USDA organic certification. Healthy Brew persisted for a couple of years but never reached significant capacity or distribution of its beers before closing.

Although no other package breweries opened, a few brewpub efforts did take root in North Texas during this time. A local Texan, Jamie Fulton, was a relatively young and avid homebrewer, hunter and sportsman and decided to follow his dream of brewing professionally with a novel brewpub concept. After graduating college, he picked up degrees from Chicago's Siebel Institute of Technology and Munich's Doemens Academy along with a pocketful of world travels. With journeyman experience at San Antonio's

Blue Star Brewing Company, Fulton paired with friend and professional chef Sean Merchant to open The Covey Restaurant and Brewery near the TCU area in April 2006.

The Covey was conceived as an alternative to the greasy-kitchen, sports-bar image of most commercial brewpubs. It offered a more upscale environment for dining and drinking with a divided space of elegant, white-tablecloth fine dining with service to match and a casual but modern bar. A brewhouse was visible behind glass between the two. Fulton focused on quality, traditional world styles of beer, served to both sides of the restaurant that also included a Covey Crew loyalty program.

The menu was especially adventurous, heavily featuring prime meats and game with a southwestern focus such as buffalo fillets, elk steaks, quail and rack of lamb as well as wood-fired pizzas, always with a certified master chef in the back. Fulton quickly became recognized for his beers, winning medals at the 2008 World Beer Cup, two at the GABF in 2009 and one again in 2010. The Covey featured periodic beer-pairing dinners and holiday specials, and Fulton even offered informal beer classes as an introduction for those curious about his ingredients and the brewing process.

Despite success as a brewery and recognition in local media as a "best of" spot for North Texas, Fulton was forced to abruptly close The Covey in September 2010, fresh off his latest medal win at the GABF. Finances were the primary reason for the closure after a couple of unprofitable years, leaving many people second-guessing the location, arguing that the original concept was better suited for a Dallas-based customer rather than suburban Fort Worth. Fulton took a position with a Canadian brewery equipment manufacturer only to return to North Texas a few years later to open Community Beer Company in Dallas.

Although no other local brewpub efforts emerged at this time, the Big Buck Brewery and Steakhouse that opened in August 2000 near Grapevine Mills Mall continued to operate until the parent Big Buck Brewery filed for bankruptcy in 2005. The Michigan-based brewery began a slow series of closures as it sold off assets, including the current Texas location. Not wanting to lose its adjoining brewpub and restaurant, neighboring recreational retailer Bass Pro Outdoor World negotiated the purchase of the brewpub and in October 2008 rebranded it as Uncle Buck's Brewery and Steakhouse. Now a North Texas operation, Uncle Buck's is still owned and operated by Bass Pro as an independent, local brewpub.

The only other brewpub activity in North Texas at this time came from outside the state as the California-based chain Gordon Biersch Brewery

Uncle Buck's Brewery and Steakhouse in Grapevine was once described as a "cathedral for steak." Housing a full, working brewery, the establishment sports a hunting lodge theme complete with animal trophies adorning the walls. *Photo by Brian Brown.*

Gordon Biersch entered the North Texas market in 2008, after establishing a franchise in Plano. *Photo by Brian Brown.*

Restaurant opened its first and only two Texas locations. The first opened in Plano in May 2008 as part of the Shops at Legacy retail development, with a second that followed in November 2009 in north Dallas across from NorthPark Center. Whereas most Gordon Biersch brewpubs adhere strictly to its established corporate styles and German brewing traditions, the two Texas stores are considered far enough out-market for the national brewpub chain that some creative leeway is granted for local brewers to deviate a bit from the standardized company recipes.

Current Texas law still strictly prohibits brewpubs from bottling their product and entering the commercial distribution system. However, Gordon Biersch not only operates a nationwide brand of brewpubs but also opened a production brewery in 1997 in San Jose, California, that bottles the same recipes offered in its national brewpubs. First distributing to Texas at about the same time as the Dallas-area brewpubs opened, Gordon Biersch became the only brewpub in the state at that time with bottled products available on retail shelves.

14
MODERN CRAFT BREWING (2011–PRESENT)

Almost overnight, the North Texas brewing scene changed dramatically in 2012. After more than a decade of no breweries operating anywhere within Dallas County, the Dallas area went from zero to dozens of microbreweries in just a few short, dramatic years. A similar pattern was reflected across the state in the larger metro areas of Houston, Austin and San Antonio, and the trend even reached into the more rural areas of West and Central Texas with small communities hours away from the urban centers.

The years immediately prior to this burst of business activity may provide some insight as to its motivation and origins. The Texas legislature was lobbied heavily in 2009 and 2011 (and again in 2013) by a grassroots movement of the commercial brewing and retail communities to relax some of the restrictive laws surrounding the operating of the state's microbreweries and brewpubs and to amend some of the stringent—and sometimes absurd—requirements for label approval for new beers. At particular issue were two key limitations, one of breweries selling direct to the public and one of brewpubs bottling and entering the standard wholesale distribution system.

More directly, Dallas experienced an effort in the summer of 2010 to get rid of the confounding local-option laws within its city limits. A holdover from Prohibition, local-option voting allowed municipal precincts and unincorporated county areas to individually vote themselves wet or dry (or something in between) for alcohol sales in bars, restaurants and retailers. This produced a patchwork of commercial restrictions across the city that

Founder John Reardon (center, plaid shirt) and the Deep Ellum Brewing Company crew celebrate the release of Four Swords at Goodfriend Beer Garden and Burger House on December 17, 2013. The beer, a Belgian-style quad, went on to win a bronze medal at the 2014 World Beer Cup. *Photo by Tyler Short, Deep Ellum Brewing Company.*

Founder Michael Peticolas (center) leads his crew in a victory pose outside the Peticolas Brewing Company in the Dallas Design District. *Photo by Brian Brown.*

sometimes varied block by block and provided no end of difficulties for distributors and start-up microbreweries.

On top of the local-option laws, the City of Dallas had a maze of illogical zoning restrictions for industrial manufacturing, made even more unworkable given that the items being manufactured were alcoholic products for human consumption. The city code was wholly unsuited and unprepared for brewing despite the city's history, permitting brewing in spaces next to hazardous materials storage and production while simultaneously classifying beer as a food product with its own set of consumer regulations. Fort Worth and McKinney had no such regulatory problems, and breweries in those respective cities were thriving. It would take strong proactive lobbying by several of the initial start-up microbreweries in Dallas to make the environment suitable for their businesses.

Accompanying these legal efforts was some consolidation of craft beer wholesalers and distributors that streamlined the process for out-of-state brewers to bring their products into Texas. Fort Worth–based Ben E. Keith Beverages was the largest Anheuser-Busch distributor in North Texas since Prohibition, and it subsequently acquired C.R. Goodman Distribution and Authentic Distributing in 2008 and Glazers in 2009 to vastly expand its state and national (as well as significant imported) craft beer portfolio. With the commercial weight of this company working with new and established craft beer brands, rapid access to new state and national breweries accelerated almost weekly.

WITH SEVERAL BREWERIES in the planning stages simultaneously, a race was on to be the first to open within the city limits of Dallas in more than a decade. The first new microbrewery to officially open in Dallas was Deep Ellum Brewing Company in October 2011. Founder John Reardon, with managing partners Scott Frieling and Jim Piel, hired Andrew (Drew) Huerter away from Missouri breweries Schlafly Tap Room and Bottleworks and Mattingly Brewing to open as their initial brewer. In 2013, they hired Jeremy Hunt, formerly of Dogfish Head Craft Brewery, as head brewer when Huerter left for his own Dallas brewpub venture.

A self-appointed "craft beer evangelist," Reardon's idea for Deep Ellum Brewing was to reflect the artistic and independent nature of the Deep Ellum arts district where he opened the brewery. The beers produced by Huerter—a lifelong homebrewer, equally passionate about creative brewing—reflected traditional styles with an unexpected and sometimes irreverent twist to place their signature brand on the flavor. Beginning even before officially

Founder Wim Bens (far right) and the employees of the Lakewood Brewing Company gather for a photo that was included in a thank-you card sent to supporters to commemorate the brewery's first anniversary. *Courtesy of the Lakewood Brewing Company.*

With an underlying beer that is said to "pair well with sin," Lakewood's Bourbon Barrel Temptress has fast become one of North Texas's most sought after brews. *Photo by Craig Bradley, Lakewood Brewing Company.*

opening the brewery, Deep Ellum Brewing embraced its adopted area with sponsored barbeques to promote its beer, homebrewing competitions and weekly brewery tours featuring local musical acts.

Fresh on the heels of Deep Ellum Brewing came Dallas's second new microbrewery, Peticolas Brewing Company, which opened in December 2011. Wholly owned and operated by Michael Peticolas, a longtime Dallas resident, lawyer and avid homebrewer, he made the jump from his family's law firm to his own small brewery, at first employing only himself (or family members) for all operations. His compact brewery was set up in an industrial park on the west side of Dallas, not too far from the new Meddlesome Moth and the growing Design District opposite downtown.

In searching for a Dallas location for his brewery, Michael went to the city council itself and asked for the best recommendation. Although suitable for his business, the industrial area suggested to Peticolas included restrictions against the manufacture of alcohol—a restriction he discovered only through his own research as an attorney. Michael filed an amendment permitting his brewery to open on the suggested site, and his legal expertise has also proven valuable to other brewers in Dallas as they worked to change the city's outdated codes.

Rounding out this initial triad of new Dallas breweries, Lakewood Brewing Company opened in August 2012. Although Belgian by birth, owner Win Bens grew up in the Dallas/Fort Worth Metroplex and, as a longtime homebrewer, dreamed of leaving his career in advertising for one in microbrewing. Bens is a graduate of the American Brewers Guild and worked for a short time at Fort Worth's Rahr & Sons before committing to his own independent brewing operations.

Together with business partner Trevor Pulver, Bens initially wanted to open a microbrewery in Dallas's Lakewood area. However, finding the property too expensive and legally restrictive for brewing purposes, he settled for a location in an industrial park in nearby Garland just over the city limits. With a very successful and fast-growing brewery serving the east side of Dallas, Lakewood Brewing produces traditional favorite beer styles with a Belgian influence as well as some Belgian-inspired special releases.

Even with a rising number of production breweries opening, the Dallas brewpub market remained disproportionately underserved. The only attempt at brewpub brewing came from the new craft beer bar, Union Bear, opening in the West Village development of Uptown Dallas in February 2012. A project of local restaurateur Matt Spillers, the split-level bar featured dozens of taps of craft beer paired with a menu of sandwiches and pizzas along with select small-batch "nanobrewery" beers starting in August 2013. It quickly ran through a succession of semi-professional brewers before abandoning the in-house brewing concept to focus simply on its retail beer and kitchen sales.

The lone brewpub effort in Fort Worth during this time came in the form of an Italian engineer named Carlo Galotto, recently retired from aerospace manufacturer Lockheed Martin. An amateur homebrewer, Galotto had a dream of opening the Zio Carlo Magnolia Brew Pub along Fort Worth's historic Magnolia Avenue to brew local craft beer and serve authentic Italian-style pizzas. Beginning development by himself in 2008, his establishment did eventually open in 2011 only serving commercial beers but not without several years of serious financial and logistical problems (for example, his chosen location in an old dry cleaners required an EPA-level cleanup) that also included a rather public meltdown on social media.

In August 2012, Galotto brought in new partners, Adam Gonzales and Austin Jones, to help construct, manage and direct his brewpub to a successful operation. Gonzales was formerly of Austin's Independence Brewing and Jones once worked as a brewer at nearby Rahr & Sons, and both brought critical commercial brewing, marketing and business experience that Galotto desperately needed. Piecing together brewing equipment, Zio Carlo began serving food in 2013 with craft brewpub beers as time, money and the function of its equipment allowed.

Farther out from the Dallas and Fort Worth urban areas, several other nearby ventures were caught in the North Texas brewing orbit. Immediately east of Dallas in Rockwall County, FireWheel Brewing Company opened in Rowlett in July 2012. Founder and Dallas native Brad Perkinson was relatively new to brewing after being introduced to the passion of craft beer at Munich's Oktoberfest celebration in 2009. With only a couple of years of homebrewing experience, he made the leap to professional, small-scale brewing after being laid off from his job as a financial analyst.

About an hour southeast of Dallas in the small town of Seven Points on the Cedar Creek Reservoir, Jim Elliot and Damon Lewis started Cedar Creek Brewery in July 2012. Originally planned for the nearby city of Kemp in Kaufman County, they elected to relocate to Seven Points entirely rather than go through a lengthy fight for permits and zoning. Initially working with leftover dairy tanks as fermenters, Cedar Creek unexpectedly gained attention in October 2013 when its Belgian-style dubbel—an overlooked, limited-release beer few even in Dallas had tried—won a gold medal at the Great American Beer Festival less than a year after it opened.

Union Bear's first house-brewed beer was a black ale called Trinity. It was crafted in the spirit of Guinness but with a lighter approach meant to enhance drinkability. *Photo by Brian Brown.*

Carlo Galotto began working in 2008 to make the Zio Carlo Magnolia Brew Pub a reality. His efforts finally paid off when he opened the establishment in October 2011. *Photo by Brian Brown.*

Left: Founder Brad Perkinson urges you to enjoy F*ing Beer, which is short for FireWheel Brewing beer. *Photo by Brian Brown.*

Below: Nearly everything you see in FireWheel's brewery was built by Perkinson, including these handmade wooden tap handles. *Photo by Brian Brown.*

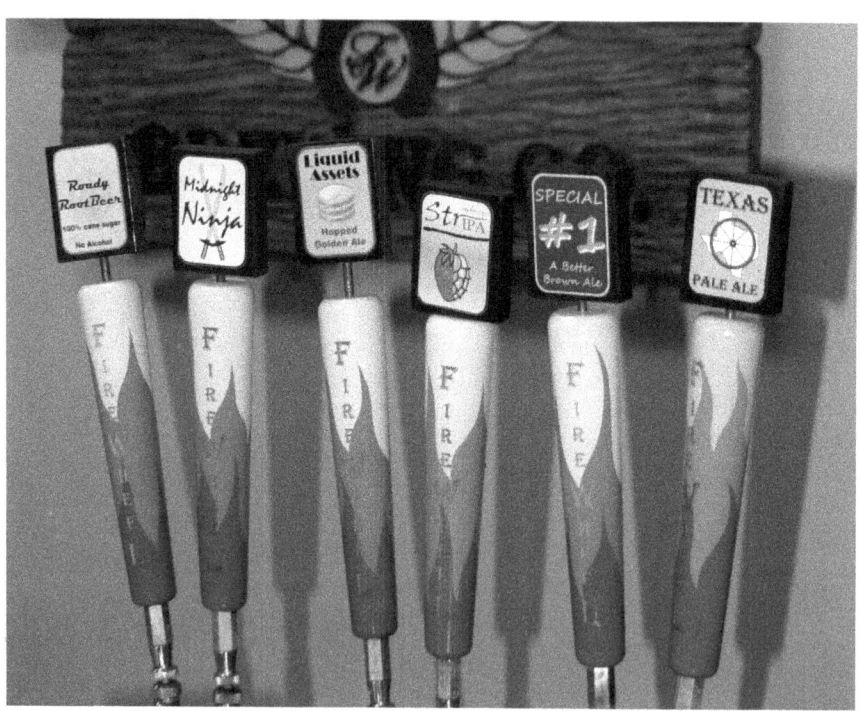

Dankosaurus, Cedar Creek's fourth year-round beer, is an East Texas homage to West Coast–style IPAs. *Photo by Blake Morrison, Cedar Creek Brewery.*

Master brewer Grant Wood (left) toasts Revolver father-and-son founders Ron and Rhett Keisler outside their brewery in Granbury. *Courtesy of Revolver Brewing Company.*

Revolver's name was inspired by the 1847 Colt Walker single-action revolver that was designed by Samuel Hamilton Walker, a Texas Ranger captain, and firearms inventor Samuel Colt. *Photo by Bryan Kaeser.*

Another outlying microbrewery opened in September 2012 in Granbury, about forty-five minutes southwest of Fort Worth. Finishing sixteen years as senior brewing manager at the Boston Beer Company (makers of Samuel Adams), North Texas native Grant Wood decided to leave New England and return home to open the Texas-themed Revolver Brewing Company near the Pecan Plantation subdivision. With projects such as BBC's Millennium and Utopia on his resume, Wood's return to Texas marked the most prominent shift in the state's craft brewing credibility since Pierre Celis.

In June 2012, the Dallas City Council unanimously voted for the proposed changes in its zoning laws for breweries, wineries and distilleries. With not even a full year since the opening of the first new brewery in Dallas, Four Corners Brewing Company became the next microbrewery to open in September 2012. Four Corners opened in a refurbished semi-trailer truck garage as part of the new Trinity Groves development in north Oak Cliff just across the Trinity River from downtown. The project of local restaurant magnate Phil Romano, Trinity Groves was planned as a fifteen-acre dining and entertainment district in west Dallas.

Four Corners Brewing was founded by homebrew hobbyists George Esquivel, Steve Porcari and Greg Leftwich, who were personally instrumental in that 2012 city council vote for Dallas's zoning rules changes in favor of small brewing operations even before they opened their own brewery. They employed award-winning local John Sims as their head brewer, himself having more than twenty years' involvement in various long-defunct Dallas breweries and brewpubs as far back as Yegua Creek and Copper Tank. (Sims is also known as a skilled brewery engineer, designing and selling custom brewing systems for places such as Union Bear.)

The next brewery to open in Dallas was Community Beer Company in January 2013. Securing a prominent site directly across the highway from the American Airlines Center and Dallas's downtown, former Fort Worth brewer Jamie Fulton brought his award-winning skills and assistant brewer Aric Hulsey from The Covey brewpub, which had closed just three years earlier. With Hulsey landing at Austin brewpub Uncle Billy's on Lake Travis, Fulton and Hulsey returned to North Texas in a big way in a partnership with former software litigator Kevin Carr.

Having previously worked for Canadian brewing equipment manufacturer Newlands Systems, Fulton outfitted his new seven-thousand-square-foot brewery with a state-of-the-art brewhouse that had the unique bonus of being the only climate-controlled brewery in North Texas. Fulton quickly returned

Founders George Esquivel, Steve Porcari and Greg Leftwich, along with brewmaster John Sims (left to right), host an event on March 3, 2012, to thank friends, family and investors after the Four Corners Brewing Company secured its location in west Dallas. *Courtesy of Steve Porcari, Four Corners Brewing Company.*

The colorfully painted side of Four Corners Brewing, part of Dallas's Trinity Groves developing social and entertainment district. *Photo by Paul Hightower.*

A Full-Bodied History of Brewing in Dallas, Fort Worth and Beyond

The Community Beer Company team, Mike DeMarco, Aric Hulsey, Jamie Fulton and founder Kevin Carr (left to right), celebrates the brewery's debut tapping of Public Ale at the Meddlesome Moth on January 16, 2013. *Courtesy of Kevin Carr, Community Beer Company.*

to form, with Community Beer winning a gold medal at the GABF in 2013 less than a year after opening. One of the first taprooms in Dallas opened at Community shortly afterward, taking advantage of recent legislative changes in the summer of 2013 that allowed limited brewery sales direct to the public.

After the opening of Community Beer in Dallas, 2013 saw an increasing acceleration in new microbrewery ventures across the Metroplex. After a gap of eight years, a second brewery, Martin House Brewing Company, opened in Fort Worth in March 2013. With a site in an industrial park overlooking the Trinity Trails floodplain and the east side of downtown, local owners and brewers Cody Martin, Dave Wedemeier and Adam Myers took their backgrounds in environmental engineering and applied that expertise to their homebrewing passion to start their own microbrewery.

Armadillo Ale Works began in 2013 in Denton with owners and brewers Yianni Arestis and Bobby Mullins. Without a brewery of its own, Armadillo chose to partner with Deep Ellum Brewing to have its recipes contract-brewed, bottled and distributed by the established Dallas microbrewery. Armadillo has already finalized plans to move its entire operations to its own Denton-based facility to open by 2015.

In June 2013, 903 Brewers opened far north of Dallas in Sherman with owners and brewers Jeremy and Natalie Roberts. Located in the area code

Left: Martin House co-founders Cody Martin (left) and David Wedemeier (right) stand outside the Flying Saucer in Fort Worth prior to their launch party there on March 30, 2013. *Courtesy of the Martin House Brewing Company.*

Below: Pac-Man is readied for a move to Martin House Brewing by co-founder Adam Myers. The cold liquor tank was acquired from Southern Star Brewing in Conroe, Texas, where it had been after previously being used by Real Ale Brewing in Blanco. *Courtesy of the Martin House Brewing Company.*

Top: Jeremy and Natalie Roberts are the husband-and-wife team behind 903 Brewers in Sherman. *Courtesy of 903 Brewers.*

Left: Roo's Red Ale from 903 Brewers is named for the kangaroo mascot of Austin College, a school located in the same town as the brewery in Sherman. *Photo by Jeremy Roberts, 903 Brewers.*

Founder Gary Humble, head brewer Caton Orrell and assistant brewer Jon Powell (left to right) make up the Grapevine Craft Brewery team. *Photo by Brian Brown.*

Grapevine's Lakefire Rye Pale Ale has a name inspired by the fire-lit skies seen by visitors to Lake Grapevine during Friday night fireworks shows in the summer. *Photo by Brian Brown.*

Rabbit Hole founders Matt Morriss, Tom Anderson and Laron Cheek (left to right) raise a glass and declare they are ready to make beer. One day later, they brewed their first batch on November 13, 2013. *Photo by Bill Castleman.*

that inspired its name, the brewery was established in a historic, century-old building that was once used as a cotton warehouse. In April 2014, the brewery began working on a long-term expansion project, which included an initial increase to a seven-barrel brewhouse and the planned addition of a bottling line to be up and running by late summer.

Grapevine Craft Brewery opened in November 2013 while operating out of a temporary location in Farmers Branch. Founder Gary Humble made the decision to begin outside the city due to construction delays on the brewery's permanent home in Grapevine (slated to begin construction in September 2014). He also wanted to make good on a pledge to have beer in the hands of supporters by the end of 2013. For his head brewer, Humble brought in Caton Orrell, whose experience included over ten years at the Boulevard Brewing Company of Kansas City, Missouri.

Rabbit Hole Brewing Company opened in December 2013 in Justin, north of Fort Worth, with owners and brewers Matt Morriss, Tom Anderson and Laron Cheek. Award-winning homebrewers and passionate hockey fans, their initial interest in brewing professionally came through custom brewing a Kölsch-style ale for Hully and Mo, an Uptown Dallas restaurant owned by former Dallas Stars center Mike Modano. Modano's interest in their amateur brewing efforts led to investing in their start-up brewery filled with Lewis Carroll references, where their 561 Kölsch-style ale is named in honor of Modano's career goals record.

15
A STILL-EVOLVING HISTORY
(2013-ONWARD)

At the time of this publication in 2014, the North Texas local brewing industry is in a state of rapid growth and flux, the same as other metro areas in the state. Historical and contemporary investigation into this topic is a work of compilation from hundreds of sources, some published and some first-person accounts. Regrettably, for simple practical reasons, an arbitrary cut was made in the narrative of this history that may not reflect some of the more recent developments in the lag between research and reading.

In an effort to be as complete as possible and leave none of our newest brewing ventures unaccounted, this chapter lists the most recent microbreweries in the Dallas, Fort Worth and Denton areas. Some are already packaging and selling beer commercially, whereas others may still be in the late planning stages, and most do not have enough of a history yet to relate in detail. However, our work would not be complete without at least an acknowledgement of their good efforts, intentions and future inclusion in updates of this work.

NORTH TEXAS BREWER Gavin Secchi and his brother, Gianni, are developing 3 Nations Brewing. Having spent time working in four separate breweries around the country, including Rahr & Sons in Fort Worth and Franconia in McKinney, the "three nations" reference stems from Secchi's exposure to the Belgian, German and English brewing traditions during the course of his career.

Audacity Brew House plans a taphouse and full-production brewery to open in Denton in summer 2014 with owner Scott Lindsey and brewer Doug Smith, both of whom relocated to Texas from Colorado. For Lindsey, the move meant a return to the city where he attended college, whereas Smith was coming off a seven-year stint as head brewer at the Fort Collins Brewery.

Bearded Eel Brewing Company plans to open in summer 2014 in Fort Worth with owners and brewers B.J. and Becky Burnett. The former educators left their jobs in 2013 to pursue their dream of opening a brewery in the community where they both grew up. The company's name is an anagram of "leaded beer," a phrase the couple uses to describe a good, strong brew.

Bitter Sisters Brewing Company plans to open in summer 2014 in Addison. Owner and brewer Matt Ehringer got his start in the late 1990s at Coach's Brewpub in Norman, Oklahoma. After four years in Norman, he worked outside the industry for a time before he and members of his family came together to start their current microbrewery business. In recognition of Ehringer's family, the brewery is named after his wife and her two sisters.

BrainDead Brewing Company plans to open in fall 2014 in Dallas's Deep Ellum entertainment district, not too far from the current Deep Ellum Brewing. BrainDead Brewing brings together three notable figures of the North Texas craft beer scene: Sam Wynne (son of Shannon Wynne of Flying Saucer fame), Jeff Fryman and Drew Huerter (formerly of Deep Ellum Brewing).

Collective Brewing Project opened in June 2014 while operating out of a temporary location in Haltom City. Partners and longtime friends Ryan Deyo and Mike Goldfuss were eyeing a late summer opening for their permanent space in the Near Southside District of Fort Worth. Hoping to stand out among the current crowd, the brewery plans to bottle and release a line of sour beers.

Cobra Brewing Company opened in December 2013 in the Old Town district of Lewisville. The family-owned and operated business consists of Bill and Sharon Shaw along with their daughter, Danielle, and her husband, Neil MacCuish. The group hopes to develop their facility as a local gathering place by offering exclusives available only at the brewery.

Dank Dog Brewing Company plans to open in late 2014 in Fort Worth with founders Justin and Laura Krey. In addition to a desire to provide great craft beer to the Metroplex, one of the brewery's guiding principles is a commitment to supporting local animal rescues.

Dead Cowboy Brewing Company plans to open sometime in 2015. Founders David and Michelle Muckian are looking to establish a farmhouse

Bill Shaw (left) and son-in-law Neil MacCuish (right) intend to incorporate homegrown hops provided by MacCuish's parents in New York into Cobra's brews. *Photo by Chris Graves.*

brewery in Rockwall County, east of Dallas, where they will grow their own fresh ingredients for use in specialty beers.

Four Bullets Brewery plans to open in late 2014 in Richardson with owners and brewers Jeff Douglas and Andrew Smeeton offering a line of traditional English-style ales. Smeeton was born and raised in England, and their brand identity is forged from Douglas's fondness for poker. "Four bullets" refers to a poker hand of four aces, and names for the brewery's products are expected to tap into phrases from other popular games as well.

Frisco City Grainworks plans to open in Frisco in late 2014 as part of a development near Toyota Stadium. A longtime resident of the area, David Clark founded the company and hired Jonny Daylett as head brewer. Daylett graduated from the American Brewers Guild in 2013, after which he apprenticed at Four Corners Brewing Company.

Hallertau Brewing Company plans to open in late 2014 in or near Frisco. Owner and brewer Don Tedlock intends to focus exclusively on strong, barrel-aged beers targeting the craft beer connoisseur.

Hemisphere Brewing Company plans to open in late 2014 on the east side of the Metroplex, with owner and brewer Brandon Mullins along with partners Jordan Ray and Robert Duke.

Independent Ale Works opened in March 2013 in Krum, a small town northwest of Denton, with owners and brewers David Miller and Stefen Windham. The brewery's location in Krum came as a compromise as a suitable site could not be found in Denton, their first choice of location.

Kirin Court, an established Richardson dim sum restaurant, quietly began serving its own house-brewed beers and custom drinks made by amateur homebrewer Lymon Liu in 2014.

Little Elm Brewing Company is still under development as a family operation with owners Danny Cirksena, Ben Cirksena and owner-brewer Nick Cirksena.

Opposite, top: Stefen Windham and David Miller established Independent Ale Works in Krum with one goal in mind—to deliver complex, unpretentious brews suitable for everyday enjoyment. *Courtesy of the* Denton Record-Chronicle.

Opposite, bottom: The Malai Kitchen's line of regionally inspired brews includes Bia Hoi, a traditional Vietnamese rice lager, and Thai-P-A, an IPA infused with Thai herbs. *Photo by Brian Brown.*

INDEPENDENT
HAND-CRAFTED,
INGREDIENTS
DOING:
WWW.INDYALES

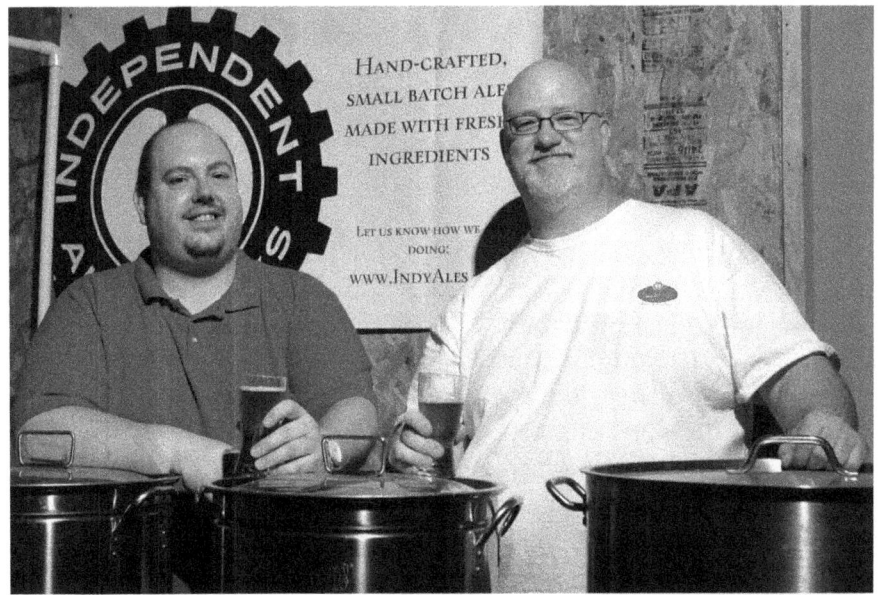

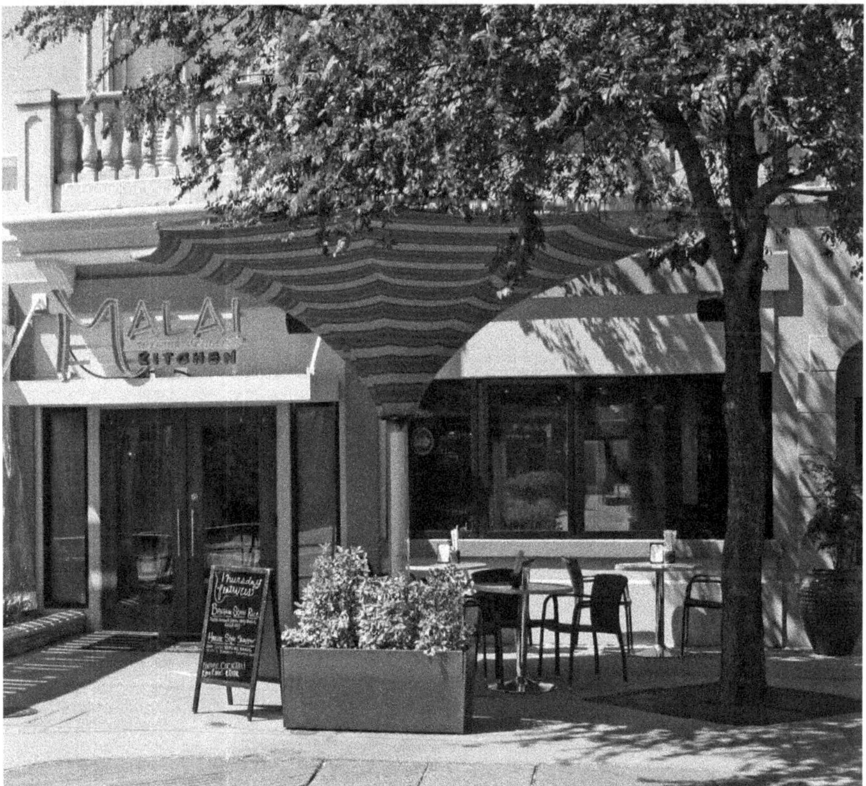
MALAI
KITCHEN

Malai Kitchen opened in the West Village area of Dallas in 2011 prior to obtaining a brewpub license and began brewing operations in March 2014. Owners Braden and Yasmin Wages had a desire to serve house beers of Southeast Asian influence that would pair well with the restaurant's cuisine. Unable to find a brewer willing to produce their recipes at small volumes, they decided to do it themselves.

Nine Band Brewing Company plans to open in late 2014 in Allen. Owner Keith Ashley, a former financial partner with Franconia Brewing, joined with local brewer Jack Sparks, who most recently worked for Saya Beer in La Paz, Bolivia. Nine Band Brewing received $75,000 in economic incentives from the City of Allen to locate its brewery within the city limits.

Noble Rey Brewing Company plans to open in late 2014 in the Oak Cliff area of south Dallas with owner and brewer Chris Rigoulot, a graduate of the American Brewers Guild from 2012 who spent time gaining experience as an apprentice at Lakewood Brewing Company.

Oak Highlands Brewing Company plans to open in late 2014 with founders Brad Mall and Derrin Williams. The brewery is expected to be established in the Lake Highlands area of east Dallas.

Old Texas Brewing Company opened in May 2013 in Burleson, south of Fort Worth. It began initially as a casual southwestern restaurant with brewing operations still pending.

On Rotation plans to open as a craft beer bar and brewpub in the Lakewood area of east Dallas sometime in 2014. Owners Jacob and Lindsay Sloan will brew small-batch beers with a variety of experimental flavors in their self-described "craft beer laboratory."

Panther Island Brewing Company opened in June 2014 after taking over the Fort Worth site formerly occupied by Great Grains and the Texas Beer Company. Owners Michael Harper and Ryan McWhorter chose the name based on a plan by the Trinity River Vision Authority to create an urban waterfront community called Panther Island, which would surround the brewery once complete.

Shannon Brewing Company plans to open in summer 2014 in Keller with owner and brewer Shannon Carter. The brewery is being built on land shared with Samantha Springs, a local source of natural spring water. Carter secured the rights to brew with the water from the springs, forming the foundation for his line of fire-brewed Irish ales.

Small Brewpub plans to open in summer 2014 in the Oak Cliff area of south Dallas. Dan Bowman and Aaron Garcia are among a group of five founders involved in the project, which is part of the Jefferson Tower

The Twin Peaks Brewing Company produces "mancrafted" beers like Dirty Blonde, Gold Digger and Knotty Brunette. *Photo by Brian Brown.*

redevelopment initiative. The establishment is expected to house a music venue in addition to the brewery as well as a full-service restaurant.

Social Brewing Company plans to open in 2015 in Fort Worth with owners and brewers Matt Morales and Brad Morian.

Steam Theory Brewing Company plans to open as a brewpub in spring 2015. Owners Jonathan Barrows and Chuck Homola expect to be located in the Lower Greenville neighborhood of Dallas.

The Texas Ale Project (originally Reunion Brewing Company) plans to open in late summer 2014 in Dallas. Founders Brent and Kat Thompson along with David and Shelley Smith lured brewer Jan Matysiak away from Sixpoint Brewery in Brooklyn, New York. Matysiak spent a part of his early career at the Live Oak Brewing Company of Austin.

The Addison-based "breastaurant" chain, Twin Peaks, opened its own brewing operation at its North Irving location in late 2013 with brewer Tom Janik, formerly of Humperdinks. Previously contract-brewed by Franconia Brewing, the brewery will supply its house beers to all of its North Texas locations.

Ugly Rugger Brewing is still under development as a Denton-area brewpub with owners and brewers Derrick and Summer Rima.

APPENDIX A
CHRONOLOGY

1857		Jean Monduel establishes the first brewery in Dallas (closing date unknown).
1859		Wheeler's brewery opens in Cedar Springs (closing date unknown).
1863		Nathaniel Terry constructs first brewery in Fort Worth (closing date unknown).
1868		John Geupel opens Cleburne Brewery in Johnson County.
1869	September	Francisca Jetzer opens brewery in Dallas. Simon Mayer opens brewery in Fort Worth.
1870		Lewis and William Van Grinderbeck operate Dallas City Brewery.

Appendix A

1871		Charles Meisterhans takes charge of Jetzer's brewery after their marriage.
		Mayer's brewery in Fort Worth closes.
1872	February	Dallas City Brewery closes.
1875		Cleburne Brewery is sold and renamed Guffee Brothers (later Guffee and Guffee).
		Euste and Meyer operate brewery at 812 Bryan Street in Dallas.
		Meisterhans's brewery closes.
1878	February	John Guffee assumes full control of Guffee and Guffee.
	November	Guffee's brewery closes.
		Brewery at 812 Bryan Street is sold and renamed E. Arnoldi & Co.
		W.F. Both & Co. operate a brewery in Weatherford (closing date unkown).
1879		E. Arnoldi & Co. closes.
1885		Anton Wagenhauser opens first industrial-scale brewery in Dallas.
1886	April	Wagenhauser's brewery sold at auction to Frederick Wolf.
	June	Wolf transfers ownership of Wagenhauser brewery to James J. and John J. Gannon.
	October	Gannon brothers charter Dallas Brewing Company.

APPENDIX A

1891	May	Texas Brewing Company opens as largest industrial enterprise in Fort Worth.
		Wagenhauser's Dallas Weiss Beer Brewery opens.
1893	February	Dallas Brewing Company sold and renamed Dallas Brewery.
1894		Simon Mayer's Berliner Weiss Beer Brewery opens in Dallas.
1898		Wagenhauser's Dallas Weiss Beer Brewery closes.
1899		Mayer's Berliner Weiss Beer Brewery closes.
1900	October	C.H. Huvelle opens brewery in Dallas.
1901	January	Excelsior Weiss Beer Brewery opens in Dallas.
		C.H. Huvelle closes.
	August	Mayer & Bruce opens in Dallas.
	December	Mayer & Bruce closes.
		Excelsior Weiss Beer Brewery closes.
1908	April	Mingus Brewing Company opens in Palo Pinto County.
1909		Mingus Brewing Company closes.
1918	March	Texas votes to ratify Eighteenth Amendment to enact Prohibition.
		Dallas Brewery closes.
		Texas Brewing closes.

Appendix A

1920	January	National Prohibition goes into effect.
1930	October	Dallas Brewery buildings torn down.
1933	August	Texas votes to ratify Twenty-first Amendment to repeal Prohibition.
		Texans approve law allowing beer containing up to 3.2 percent alcohol by weight.
	October	Superior Brewing Company opens in Fort Worth.
1934	March	Schepps Brewing Corporation opens in Dallas.
	July	A new Dallas Brewery opens.
1939	February	Dallas Brewery closes.
	June	Schepps Brewing reorganized as Time Brewing Incorporated.
1940		Superior Brewing closes.
1941		Time Brewing sold and renamed Dallas–Fort Worth Brewing Company.
1951		Dallas–Fort Worth Brewing closes.
1963	January	Carling Brewing begins construction of Fort Worth plant.
1965	May	Carling Brewing opens Fort Worth brewing facility.
	October	Carling's Fort Worth brewery closes "temporarily."
1966		Miller Brewing buys Carling's Fort Worth plant.

Appendix A

1969	June	Miller begins brewing at renovated Fort Worth location.
1973	November	Texas Brewing Company buildings torn down. Miller test-markets a new low-calorie product, Miller Lite.
1975	January	Miller releases Miller Lite commercially, brewed at its Fort Worth brewery.
1981		Richland Beverage Corporation opens in Dallas making non-alcoholic beer.
1982		Reinheitsgebot Brewing Company legally opens in Plano.
1983		Texas legalizes homebrewing of beer and wine.
1985		Reinheitsgebot Brewing sells its first beers commercially.
1988	May	Addison Brewing opens in Addison.
1989	March	West End Brewing/Dallas Brewing opens in Dallas.
	August	Addison Brewing closes.
1990	June	Miller upgrades its Fort Worth facility for production of Miller Genuine Draft. Reinheitsgebot Brewing closes.

Appendix A

1991		Humperdinks Restaurant and Brewery opens in Richardson.
1992		Miller's Fort Worth site becomes its largest United States brewery.
1993	August	Texas legalizes and licenses brewpubs.
		Dallas Brewing reorganized as Texas Brewing Company.
1994	January	Yegua Creek Brewing Company opens in Dallas.
	June	Hubcap Brewery and Kitchen opens in Dallas.
		St. Andrews Brewing Company opens in Dallas (closing date unknown).
1995	February	Hoffbrau Steaks and Brewery opens in Addison.
	May	Rock Bottom Brewing Company opens its second Texas location in Addison.
		TwoRows Restaurant and Brewery opens in Dallas.
	September	Hoffbrau Steaks and Brewery opens in Dallas.
		Routh Street Brewery and Grille opens in Dallas.
		Humperdinks Restaurant and Brewery opens in Arlington.
1996	January	Copper Tank Brewing Company opens in Dallas.
	February	Main Street Brewing Company opens in Dallas.
	March	Panther City Brewery and Café opens in Fort Worth.
	May	Breckinridge Brewery opens in Dallas and closes before its first year.
	August	Moon Under Water opens in Dallas and closes after only two months.
		Panther City Brewery and Café closes before the end of the year.

Appendix A

1997	March	Great Grains Brewery opens in Dallas.
		USA Café (USA Brewing Company) opens in Fort Worth.
		Schooner Brewery acquires Hubcap Brewery and Kitchen.
		Humperdinks original Dallas location opens as a brewpub after a remodel.
		Humperdinks opens a second brewpub location in Dallas.
1998	July	Main Street Brewing closes.
	September	Yegua Creek closes.
		Texas Brewing sold to other investors.
		Humperdinks Restaurant and Brewery opens in Addison.
		USA Café closes.
1999	March	GameCon, Inc. (formerly Schooner Brewery) closes Hubcap Brewery.
2000	April	Routh Street Brewery and Grille abandons brewing operations, continuing as a restaurant.
		Texas Beer Company opens in Fort Worth.
	August	Big Buck Brewery and Steakhouse opens in Grapevine.
2001	October	Hoffbrau Steaks closes its Dallas and Addison brewpubs.
		Copper Tank closes.
		Rock Bottom closes.
	December	Texas Beer Company closes.

Appendix A

2003		BJ's Restaurant and Brewhouse opens its first Texas location in Lewisville.
		TwoRows opens a new brewpub location in Addison.
		Healthy Brew opens in Fort Worth (closing date unknown).
2004	May	Great Grains moves operations to Fort Worth and is shut down by TABC.
	September	Rahr & Sons Brewing opens in Fort Worth.
2006	April	The Covey Restaurant and Brewery opens in Fort Worth.
		Humperdinks brewpubs reorganized as Humperdinks of Texas.
2008	February	Franconia Brewing opens in McKinney.
	May	Gordon Biersch Brewery Restaurant opens in Plano.
	October	Big Buck Brewery and Steakhouse rebranded as Uncle Buck's Brewery and Steakhouse.
		TwoRows closes its Dallas Brewpub.
2009	November	Gordon Biersch Brewery Restaurant opens in Dallas.
		TwoRows closes its Addison brewpub.
2010	February	Rahr & Sons' roof collapses from recent snowfall.
		Franconia experiences a tank rupture during a Saturday tour.
	September	The Covey closes.
2011	October	Zio Carlo Magnolia Brew Pub opens in Fort Worth.
		Deep Ellum Brewing Company opens in Dallas.
	December	Peticolas Brewing Company opens in Dallas.

Appendix A

2012	February	Union Bear opens in Dallas.
	July	Cedar Creek Brewery opens in Seven Points.
		FireWheel Brewing Company opens in Rowlett.
	August	Lakewood Brewing Company opens in Garland.
	September	Four Corners Brewing Company opens in Dallas.
		Revolver Brewing opens in Granbury.
2013	January	Armadillo Ale Works partners with Deep Ellum Brewing.
		Community Beer Company opens in Dallas.
	March	Independent Ale Works opens in Krum.
		Martin House Brewing Company opens in Fort Worth.
	June	903 Brewers opens in Sherman.
	August	Union Bear begins brewing operations but ceases after only a few months.
	November	Grapevine Craft Brewery opens temporary location in Farmers Branch.
		Twin Peaks begins brewing operations at its restaurant in Irving.
	December	Cobra Brewing Company opens in Lewisville.
		Rabbit Hole Brewing Company opens in Justin.
2014	March	Malai Kitchen begins brewing operations at its restaurant in Dallas.
	July	Collective Brewing Project opens temporary location in Haltom City.
		Panther Island Brewing Company opens in Fort Worth.
		Kirin Court begins brewing operations at its restaurant in Richardson.

Appendix B
North Texas Craft Beer Resources

Breweries

Local

Armadillo Ale Works
PO Box 3
Denton, TX 76202
Website: www.armadilloaleworks.com

Cedar Creek Brewery
244 East Cedar Creek Parkway
Seven Points, TX 75143
Website: www.cedarcreekbrewery.com

Cobra Brewing Company
146 Whatley Avenue
Lewisville, TX 75057
Website: www.cobrabrewingco.com

Appendix B

The Collective Brewing Project
112 St. Louis Avenue
Fort Worth, TX 76104
Website: www.collectivebrew.com

Community Beer Company
1530 Inspiration Drive, Suite 200
Dallas, TX 75207
Website: www.communitybeer.com

Deep Ellum Brewing Company
2823 St. Louis Street
Dallas, TX 75226
Website: www.deepellumbrewing.com

FireWheel Brewing Company
3313 Enterprise Drive
Rowlett, TX 75088
Website: firewheelbrewing.com

Four Corners Brewing Company
423 Singleton Boulevard
Dallas, TX 75212
Website: fcbrewing.com

Franconia Brewing Company
495 McKinney Parkway
McKinney, TX 75071
Website: franconiabrewing.com

Grapevine Craft Brewery
924 Jean Street
Grapevine, TX 76051
Website: www.grapevineontap.com

Independent Ale Works
11555 U.S. Highway 380 West, Suite 209
Krum, TX 76249
Website: www.indyales.com

Appendix B

Lakewood Brewing Company
2302 Executive Drive
Garland, TX 75041
Website: www.lakewoodbrewing.com

Martin House Brewing Company
220 South Sylvania Avenue, Suite 209
Fort Worth, TX 76111
Website: www.martinhousebrewing.com

903 Brewers
1718 South Elm Street
Sherman, TX 75090
Website: www.903brewers.com

Panther Island Brewing
501 North Main Street
Fort Worth, TX 76164
Website: www.pantherislandbrewing.com

Peticolas Brewing Company
2026 Farrington Street
Dallas, TX 75207
Website: www.peticolasbrewing.com

Rabbit Hole Brewing Company
608 Topeka Avenue
Justin, TX 76247
Website: www.rabbitholebrewing.com

Rahr & Sons Brewing Company
701 Galveston Avenue
Fort Worth, TX 76104
Website: www.rahrbrewing.com

Revolver Brewing Company
5650 Matlock Road
Granbury, TX 76049
Website: www.revolverbrewing.com

APPENDIX B

Regional

MILLERCOORS
7001 South Freeway
Fort Worth, TX 76134
Website: www.millercoors.com

Brewpubs

GORDON BIERSCH BREWERY RESTAURANT
8060 Park Lane, Suite 125
Dallas, TX 75231

7401 Lone Star Drive, Suite B120
Plano, TX 75024
Website: www.gordonbiersch.com

HUMPERDINKS RESTAURANT AND BREWERY
(note: Addison location does not brew on-site)
3820 Belt Line Road
Addison, TX 75001

700 Six Flags Drive
Arlington, TX 76011

2208 West Northwest Highway
Dallas, TX 75220

6050 Greenville Avenue
Dallas, TX 75206
Website: www.humperdinks.com

KIRIN COURT
221 West Polk Street #200
Richardson, TX 75081
Website: www.kirincourt.com

Appendix B

Malai Kitchen
3699 McKinney Avenue #319
Dallas, TX 75204
Website: www.malaikitchen.com

Twin Peaks Brewing Company
1500 Market Place Boulevard
Irving, TX 75063
Website: www.twinpeaksrestaurant.com

Uncle Buck's Brewery and Steakhouse
2501 Bass Pro Drive
Grapevine, TX 76051
Website: restaurants.basspro.com/UncleBucksSteakhouse

Union Bear
3699 McKinney Avenue #306
Dallas, TX 75204
Website: www.unionbear.com

Zio Carlo Magnolia Brew Pub
1001 West Magnolia Avenue
Fort Worth, TX 76104
Website: www.ziocarlobrew.com

Projects in Development

Breweries

Audacity Brew House
1012 Shady Oaks Drive
Denton, TX 76205

Appendix B

Bearded Eel Craft Brewery
12509 Business Highway 287 North, Suite 210
Fort Worth, TX 76179

Bitter Sisters Brewing Company
15103 Surveyor Boulevard
Addison, TX 75001

Four Bullets Brewery
640 North Interurban Street
Richardson, TX 75081

Frisco City Grainworks
Frisco Street and Research Road
Frisco, TX 75034

Nine Band Brewing Company
9 Prestige Circle
Allen, TX 75002

Noble Rey Brewing Company
1400 East Jefferson Boulevard
Dallas, TX 75203

On Rotation
7328 Gaston Road
Dallas, TX 75214

Shannon Brewing Company
818 North Main Street
Keller, TX 76248

Texas Ale Project
1001 North Riverfront Boulevard
Dallas, TX 75207

Appendix B

Brewpubs

BRAINDEAD BREWING COMPANY
2625 Main Street
Dallas, TX 75226

OLD TEXAS BREWING COMPANY
112 West Ellison Street
Burleson, TX 76028

SMALL BREWPUB
333 West Jefferson Boulevard
Dallas, TX 75208

Homebrew Clubs

Cap and Hare Homebrew Club, Fort Worth
Website: www.capandhare.com

Dallas Homebrew Collective
Website: www.homebrewcollective.com

Denton County Homebrewers Guild
Website: www.dchg.org

Horsemen of the Hopocalypse, Fort Worth
Website: www.hopocalypse.org

Knights of the Brown Bottle, Arlington
Website: www.kobb.org

North Texas Homebrewers Association, Richardson
Website: www.nthba.org

Appendix B

Other Resources

News and Event Listings

Beer Drinker's Society
Website: beerdrinkerssociety.com

Beer in Big D
Website: www.beerinbigd.com

Dallas Brew Scene
Website: www.dallasbrewscene.com

Dallas Craft Beer Examiner
Website: www.examiner.com/craft-beer-in-dallas/paul-hightower

Dallas Morning News Craft Beer and Cocktails Blog
Website: beerblog.dallasnews.com

Fort Worth Brew Scene
Website: www.fortworthbrewscene.com

Texas Brews
Website: www.texasbrews.org

Festivals and Events

Best Little Brewfest in Texas
Website: www.bestlittlebrewfestintexas.com

Big Texas Beer Fest
Website: www.bigtexasbeerfest.com

Appendix B

Bluebonnet Brew-Off
Website: www.bluebonnetbrewoff.com

Brew Riot
Website: www.brewriot.com

Dallas Observer Brewfest
Website: microapp.dallasobserver.com/brewfest

Flying Saucer Beer Feast
Website: www.beerknurd.com

North Texas Beer and Wine Festival
Website: www.northtexasbeerfestival.com

North Texas Beer Week
Website: www.ntxbeerweek.com

Untapped Festival
Website: www.untapped-festival.com

City Tours

Dallas Brew Bus
Website: www.dallasbrewbus.com

BIBLIOGRAPHY

American Breweriana Journal. Multiple publication dates. Digital images, American Breweriana Association, http://americanbreweriana.org/.

Ancestry.com. *1860 United States Federal Census* [database online]. Provo, UT: Ancestry.com Operations, Inc., 2009. Images reproduced by FamilySearch.

———. *1870 United States Federal Census* [database online]. Provo, UT: Ancestry.com Operations, Inc., 2009. Images reproduced by FamilySearch.

———. *Texas Death Index, 1903–2000* [database online]. Provo, UT: Ancestry.com Operations Inc, 2006.

———. *U.S. City Directories, 1821–1989* [database online]. Provo, UT: Ancestry.com Operations, Inc., 2011.

———. *U.S., Find a Grave Index, 1700s–Current* [database online]. Provo, UT: Ancestry.com Operations, Inc., 2012.

———. *U.S. IRS Tax Assessment Lists, 1862–1918* [database online]. Provo, UT: Ancestry.com Operations Inc, 2008.

Arnold, John P., and Frank Penman. *History of the Brewing Industry and Brewing Science in America.* Chicago: United States Brewers Association, 1933; Reprint Edition, BeerBooks.com, 2006.

Bibliography

Atkinson, Jim, and Judy Wood. *Fort Worth's Huge Deal: Unwinding Westside's Twisted Legend.* Fort Worth, TX: Authors, 2010. University of North Texas Libraries, The Portal to Texas History, http://texashistory.unt.edu/ark:/67531/metapth244398/ (accessed June 20, 2014).

Austin American-Statesman. Multiple publication dates. Digital images. Database: The Austin American Statesman Archive.

Barnes, Larue. "Rip-roarin' Cleburne." *Cleburne Times-Review,* July 12, 2008. http://www.cleburnetimesreview.com/features/x489002996/Larue-Barnes-Rip-roarin-Cleburne (accessed June 19, 2014).

Baron, Stanley. *Brewed in America: A History of Beer and Ale in the United States.* Boston: Little, Brown & Co., 1962; Reprint Edition, BeerBooks.com, 2007.

Burns, Ken, and Lynn Novick. *Prohibition.* DVD. Co-production of Florentine Films and WETA, 2011.

Cherington, Ernest Hurst, ed. *The Anti-Saloon League Year Book.* Westerville, OH: The Anti-Saloon League of America, 1908–1922. Hathitrust Digital Library.

Collected evidence and testimony from Texas Attorney General's investigation. *The Brewers and Texas Politics, Vols. I and II.* San Antonio, TX: Passing Show Printing, 1916.

Conlon, Charles F. "Taxation in the Alcoholic Beverage Field." *Law and Contemporary Problems* 7, no. 4 (Fall 1940): 728–48. Duke Law Scholarship Repository, http://scholarship.law.duke.edu/cgi/viewcontent.cgi?article=2050&context=lcp (accessed June 19, 2014).

Cook, George. "Hidden in Plain Sight: The Story of Long's Lake." *Legacies: A History Journal for Dallas and North Central Texas* 22, no. 1 (Spring 2010): 4–14. University of North Texas, The Portal to Texas History, http://texashistory.unt.edu/ark:/67531/metapth146051/m1/6/ (accessed June 18, 2014).

Cook, Rita, and Jeffrey Yarbrough. *Prohibition in Dallas and Fort Worth: Blind Tigers, Bootleggers and Bathtub Gin.* Charleston, SC: The History Press, 2013.

BIBLIOGRAPHY

Crowell, Gwinnetta Malone. "Not in My Back Yard: 'Legalizing' Prostitution in Dallas from 1910–1913." *Legacies: A History Journal for Dallas and North Central Texas* 22, no. 2 (Fall 2010): 16–32. University of North Texas, The Portal to Texas History, http://texashistory.unt.edu/ark:/67531/metapth146050/m1/18/ (accessed June 18, 2014).

Dallas Daily Herald. 1873–1887. Digital images. University of North Texas Libraries, The Portal to Texas History, http://texashistory.unt.edu/.

Dallas Herald. 1849–1873. Digital images. University of North Texas Libraries, The Portal to Texas History, http://texashistory.unt.edu/.

Dallas Morning News. 1885–1984. Digital images. NewsBank/Readex, Database: Dallas Morning News Historical Archive.

———. 1984–Current. Digital images. NewsBank, Database: The Dallas Morning News Archive.

Dallas Observer. Multiple publication dates. Digital images. Dallas Observer Search (online), Articles and Blogs, http://www.dallasobserver.com/.

Dallas Weekly Herald. 1873–1885. Digital images. University of North Texas Libraries, The Portal to Texas History, http://texashistory.unt.edu/.

Delorantis, Kristin. "Brewed to Perfection: Alumnus Takes on Brewing Industry with New Beer." *TCU Daily Skiff*, September 20, 2000.

DFW.com. *Fort Worth Star Telegram*. http://www.dfw.com/ (accessed July 1, 2014). Multiple locations.

D Magazine. Multiple publication dates. Digital images. Search D Magazine (online), Articles/Blog Posts, http://www.dmagazine.com/.

El Paso Herald-Post. "Begin Work on Ft. Worth's First 3.2 Per Cent Brewery." June 20, 1933.

Erwin and Geupel Family Album. "Cleburne Brewery." http://erwinandgeupel.com/geupel/andrew/brewery/brewery.htm (accessed June 19, 2014).

Bibliography

Fort Worth Daily Gazette. 1882–1891. Digital images. University of North Texas Libraries, The Portal to Texas History, http://texashistory.unt.edu/.

Fort Worth Gazette. 1891–1898. Digital images. University of North Texas Libraries, The Portal to Texas History, http://texashistory.unt.edu/.

Fort Worth Morning Register. 1897–1902. Digital images. NewsBank/NewsLibrary.com, Database: Fort Worth Morning Register Historical Archive.

Fort Worth Star-Telegram. 1902–1991. Digital images. NewsBank/NewsLibrary.com, Database: Fort Worth Star Telegram Historical Archive.

———. 1991–Current. Digital images. NewsBank/NewsLibrary.com, Database: Fort Worth Star Telegram Archive.

Fort Worth Weekly Gazette. 1882–1891. Digital images. University of North Texas Libraries, The Portal to Texas History, http://texashistory.unt.edu/.

Friedrich, Manfred, and Donald Bull. *The Register of United States Breweries, 1876–1976*. Trumbull, CT: Bull, 1976.

Gannon v. Northwestern Nat. Bank, 83 Tex. 274, 18 S.W. 573 (Tex. 1892). WestLaw Campus Research (accessed June 19, 2014).

Garrett, Julia Kathryn. *Fort Worth: A Frontier Triumph*. Austin, TX: Encino Press, 1972. Reprint, Forth Worth: Texas Christian University Press, 1996.

Gould, Lewis L. "Progressive Era." *Handbook of Texas Online*. Texas State Historical Association. http://www.tshaonline.org/handbook/online/articles/npp01 (accessed July 6, 2014).

———. *Progressives and Prohibitionists: Texas Democrats in the Wilson Era*. Austin: University of Texas Press, 1973.

Griffie v. Maxey, 58 Tex. 210, 1882 WL 9601 (Tex. 1882). WestLaw Campus Research (accessed June 19, 2014).

BIBLIOGRAPHY

Guffee v. State, 8 Tex. App. 187, 1880 WL 8995 (Tex. Ct. App. 1880). WestLaw Campus Research (accessed June 19, 2014).

Hennech, Michael C., and Tracé Etienne-Gray. "Brewing Industry." *Handbook of Texas Online.* Texas State Historical Association. http://www.tshaonline.org/handbook/online/articles/dib01 (accessed June 19, 2014).

Hennech, Mike. "The Business of Brewing." *Heritage* (Spring 2005): 19–22. University of North Texas, The Portal to Texas History, http://texashistory.unt.edu/ark:/67531/metapth45370/m1/19/ (accessed June 19, 2014); crediting Texas Historical Foundation, Austin, Texas.

———. *Encyclopedia of Texas Breweries: Pre-Prohibition (1836–1918).* Irving, TX: Ale Publishing Company, 1990.

Holt, Jeff. TexasBreweries.com. http://texasbreweries.com/ (accessed June 19, 2014). Multiple locations.

Horsey, Catherine. "Dallas's Disappearing Architectural Heritage." *Legacies: A History Journal for Dallas and North Central Texas* 9, no. 2 (Fall 1997): 4–9. University of North Texas, The Portal to Texas History, http://texashistory.unt.edu/ark:/67531/metapth146051/m1/6/ (accessed June 18, 2014).

Houston Chronicle. 1985–2014. Digital images. NewsBank, Database: The Houston Chronicle Archive.

Ivy, H.A. *Rum on the Run in Texas: A Brief History of Prohibition in the Lone Star State.* Dallas, TX: Temperance Pub. Co., 1910.

Ivy, James D. *No Saloon in the Valley: The Southern Strategy of Texas Prohibitionists in the 1880s.* Waco, TX: Baylor University Press, 2003.

Kerr, K. Austin. "Prohibition." *Handbook of Texas Online.* Texas State Historical Association. http://www.tshaonline.org/handbook/online/articles/vap01 (accessed June 19, 2014).

Knight, Oliver. *Fort Worth: Outpost on the Trinity.* Norman: University of Oklahoma Press, 1953.

Makers of Fort Worth. Fort Worth, TX: Fort Worth Newspaper Artists' Association, 1914. University of North Texas Libraries, The Portal to Texas History, http://texashistory.unt.edu/ark:/67531/metapth41334/ (accessed June 19, 2014).

McDonald, William L. *Dallas Rediscovered: A Photographic Chronicle of Urban Expansion 1870–1925.* Dallas, TX: The Dallas Historical Society, 1978.

Memorial and Biographical History of Dallas County, Texas. Chicago: Lewis Publishing Company, 1892. University of North Texas Libraries, The Portal to Texas History, http://texashistory.unt.edu/ark:/67531/metapth20932/ (accessed June 20, 2014).

Miller v. Wagenhauser, 18 Mo. App. 11, 1885 WL 7527 (Mo. App. 1885). WestLaw Campus Research (accessed June 19, 2014).

Milwaukee Journal. "Brewers Fear Cork Shortage." August 10, 1941.

———. "Milwaukee Area Deaths and Funerals." December 30, 1969.

Modern Brewery Age. "Allan Barney, Brewing Industry Figure, Dies at 81." March 20, 1995.

———. "Texas Regulators Shut Down Microbrewery." July 19, 2004.

Moffatt, Lori. "Cheers to Texas Craft Breweries." *Texas Highways.* August 1995: 14–21.

Motl, Kevin C. "Under the Influence: The Texas Business Men's Association and the Campaign against Reform, 1906–1915. *The Southwestern Historical Quarterly* 109, no. 4 (April 2006): 494–529. JSTOR, http://www.jstor.org/stable/30242333 (accessed June 19, 2014).

Myers, Cindi. "What's Brewing at the Pub." *Texas Highways.* August 1995: 22–27.

National Association of Practical Refrigerating Engineers. "E. Arnoldi, Deceased." *Ice and Refrigeration Illustrated* 49, no. 5 (November 1915): 247.

Bibliography

Neville, A.W., ed. "The History of Lamar County, Chapter 23: Eben L. Dohoney." *The Paris News*, September 26, 1937: 13.

New Brewer. Multiple publication dates. Print, Brewers Association, Boulder, CO.

Otto v. Republic Nat. Co., 173 S.W.2d 245 (Tex. Civ. App. 1943). WestLaw Campus Research (accessed June 19, 2014).

Paddock. B.B., ed. *History of Texas: Fort Worth and the Texas Northwest Edition*. Vols. 1–4. Chicago: Lewis Publishing Company, 1922.

Park, Milton, ed. "Texans Take Many Prizes." *Southern Mercury* 24, no. 43, ed. 1 (Thursday, October 27, 1904): 5. University of North Texas Libraries, The Portal to Texas History, http://texashistory.unt.edu/ark:/67531/metapth186071/m1/5/ (accessed June 20, 2014).

———. "To Purify the Liquor Traffic." *Southern Mercury* 24, no. 2, ed. 1 (Thursday, January 14, 1904): 5. University of North Texas Libraries, The Portal to Texas History, http://texashistory.unt.edu/ark:/67531/metapth186030/m1/1/ (accessed June 20, 2014).

Pluta, Joseph E. *Regional Change in the U.S. Brewing Industry*. Austin: Bureau of Business research, Graduate School of Business, University of Texas at Austin, 1983.

Raines, Cadwell Walton. *Analytical Index to the Laws of Texas 1823–1905*. Austin, TX: Von Boeckmann-Jones Company, 1906.

Sacred Heart Review. "The Hepburn-Dolliver Bill." December 31, 1904.

Santerre, George H. *White Cliffs of Dallas: The Story of La Reunion, the Old French Colony*. Dallas, TX: Book Craft, 1955.

Savardan, Augustin, and Eloise Santerre. *Reunion*. Dallas, TX: Southern Methodist University, 1936.

Scientific Station for Pure Products. "The Lamsens Method of Carbonating Beer." *Pure Products* 8, no. 8 (August 1912): 409.

Selcer, Richard F. *Hell's Half Acre: The Life and Legend of a Red-Light District.* Fort Worth: Texas Christian University Press, 1991.

Siebel, J.E., ed. "Mixed Pickles." *American Chemical Review* 4, no. 9 (December 1884): 216.

Southwest Brewing News. Multiple publication dates. Digital images, Brewing News, Database: Southwest Brewing News Archives, http://www.brewingnews.com/archives/.

Superior Brewing Co. v. Curtis, 116 S.W.2d 853 (Tex. Civ. App. 1938). WestLaw Campus Research (accessed June 19, 2014).

Sutton, Jared Paul. *Ethnic Minorities and Prohibition in Texas, 1887 to 1919.* Denton, TX. UNT Digital Library. http://digital.library.unt.edu/ark:/67531/metadc5341/ (accessed June 19, 2014).

Taylor Daily Press. "Remodel Brewery at Ft. Worth." June 21, 1933.

Texas. *The Laws of Texas 1822–1897*. Vols. 1–10. Austin, TX: The Gammel Book Company, 1898.

———. *The Laws of Texas 1822–1909*. Vols. 11–14. Austin, TX: The Gammel Book Company, 1898–1909.

Texas Almanac. "Prohibition Elections in Texas." http://www.texasalmanac.com/topics/elections/prohibition-elections-texas (accessed June 19, 2014).

Van Wieren, Dale P. *American Breweries II.* West Point, PA: East Coast Breweriana Association, 1995.

Victoria Advocate. "Beer Flowing at Tiny Brewery." November 17, 1985.

Wahl, Arnold S., and Robert Wahl, eds. *American Brewers' Review*, journal, multiple publication dates; digital images, HathiTrust Digital Library, http://www.hathitrust.org/; crediting New York Public Library.

Watson, John. "Cleburne Brewery—Another Cleburne First." *Cleburne Times-Review*, June 26, 2006. http://www.cleburnetimesreview.com/features/

x488977208/John-Watson-Cleburne-brewery-another-Cleburne-first (accessed June 14, 2014).

White, Owen P. "Dripping Dry Dallas." *Collier's Weekly*, July 20, 1929: 8–9.

Wolf v. Butler, 81 Tex. 86, 16 S.W. 794 (Tex. 1891). WestLaw Campus Research (accessed June 19, 2014).

Wolf v. Butler, 8 Tex. Civ. App. 468, 28 S.W. 51 (Tex. Civ. App. 1894). WestLaw Campus Research (accessed June 19, 2014).

INDEX

A

Addison Brewing Company 96, 159
Addison, TX 96, 102, 104, 112, 148
Allen, TX 152
Anderson, E.F. 80
Anderson, Tom 145
Andrews Distributing 116
Anheuser-Busch 28, 35
Anti-Saloon League of Texas 62
Arestis, Yianni 141
Arlington, TX 103
Armadillo Ale Works 141, 163, 165
Arnoldi, Ernest 27, 28
Authentic Distributing 131

B

Barney, Allan J. 83
Bassard, John 19
Belgian influence 73, 133
Bender, Rudolph August 80, 82
Ben E. Keith Beverages 131
Bens, Wim 133
Berliner Weiss Beer Brewery 30, 157
biergartens 28, 30
Big Buck Brewery and Steakhouse 111, 125, 161, 162
BJ's Restaurant and Brewhouse 112, 162
Breckinridge Brewery 105, 160
breweries
   accidents and damage 118, 121
   first microbrewery 93
   out of state 26, 29, 33, 36, 45, 71, 87, 102, 103, 105, 111, 112, 125
   technology 34, 73, 88, 89, 91
   three-tier system 98
brewpubs
   first in North Texas 101
   legalization 98, 101
Brotzman, Mike 102
Brown, Gary 102
Burleson, TX 152
Busch, Adolphus 47, 48, 51, 64

C

Carling Brewing 87, 88, 89, 158
Carr, Kevin 139
Carroll, Patrick 102, 104
Cartwright, Rob 104
cattle industry 25
Cedar Creek Brewery 134, 163, 165
Cheatum, Joe 110

INDEX

Cheek, Laron 145
Civil War 18, 19, 21, 26
Cleburne Brewery 21, 23, 155, 156
Cleburne, TX 22, 176, 182
Cole, Jerry 96
Community Beer Company 125, 139, 166
Contreras, Joe 106
Coors Distribution 120
Copper Tank Brewing Company 104, 111, 160, 161
Corey, George 106
Correard, Greg 106
Courtney, Jason 114
Covey Restaurant and Brewery, The 125, 139, 162
C.R. Goodman Distribution 131
criminal activity
  monopolies 46
  murder 22, 60, 104
  red-light districts 54
Cromie, Rob 101, 106
Curtis, Dan E. 73, 74

D

Dallas Brewery (1893) 38, 43, 45, 46, 60, 61, 64, 66, 67, 71, 79, 85, 96, 157, 158
Dallas Brewery Incorporated (1934) 78, 79, 80, 158
Dallas Brewing Company (1886) 36, 37, 38, 48, 82, 98, 156, 157
Dallas Brewing Company (1989) 95, 96, 106, 159, 160
Dallas City Brewery 19, 155, 156
Dallas–Fort Worth Brewing Company 81, 82, 83, 84, 85, 158
Dallas, TX
  biergartens 28, 29, 30
  breweries 18, 19, 22, 26, 27, 30, 33, 36, 38, 43, 76, 81, 99, 106, 110, 131, 133, 139, 152, 153
  brewpubs 101, 102, 103, 104, 105, 127, 133, 148, 152, 153

first brewery 17
founding of 17
La Reunion colony 18, 19, 27, 28
railroads 25
Dallas Weiss Beer Brewery 35, 157
Deemer, Tim 102
Deep Ellum Brewing Company 131, 133, 141, 148, 162, 166
Denison, TX 25, 26
Denton, TX 141, 148, 153
Dixon, Mike 22, 23
Dohoney, Ebeneezer Lafayette 56, 58, 59
Dray, Allan 96, 98, 99

E

E. Arnoldi & Co. 27, 33, 156
Eighteenth Amendment (Prohibition) 65, 70, 157
Elliot, Jim 134
Esquivel, George 139
Euste, C. 27, 156
Excelsior Weiss Beer Brewery 43, 157

F

Farmers Branch, TX 145
Feickert, Adolph 30, 47
FireWheel Brewing Company 134, 163, 166
Flowers, J.B. 114, 116
Flying Saucer Draught Emporium 106
Formby, Tony 116, 118
Fort Worth, TX
  breweries 21, 38, 71, 88, 111, 114, 124, 141, 148, 153
  brewpubs 104, 107, 125, 134, 152
  cattle industry 25
  first brewery 21
  founding of 20, 21
  railroads 25
Four Corners Brewing Company 139, 150, 163, 166
Francois, Mark 104

INDEX

Franconia Brewing Company 121, 123, 147, 152, 153, 162, 166
French influence 18
Frieling, Scott 131
Frisco, TX 150
Fulton, Jamie 124, 125, 139

G

Galotto, Carlo 134
Gannon, James J. 36, 37, 38, 41, 48, 156
Gannon, John J. 36, 37, 156
Gannon, R.C. 36
Garland, TX 133
German influence
  after Prohibition 80, 113, 121
  before Prohibition 21, 22, 28, 33
  North Texas 28
  state settlement 26
Geupel, John Andrew 21, 22, 155
Ginger Man 106
Glazers 131
Gonzales, Adam 134
Gordon Biersch Brewery Restaurant 127, 162, 168
Granbury, TX 139
Grapevine Craft Brewery 145, 163, 166
Grapevine, TX 125, 145
Great Grains Brewery 110, 111, 112, 152, 161, 162
Grinderbeck, Lewis 19, 155
Guffee and Guffee 156
Guffee Brothers Brewery 22, 156
Guffee, Elijah 22, 23
Guffee, John 22, 23, 156

H

Hahn, Frank 82
Hahn, Paul H. 82
Haltom City, TX 148
Harbin, Ken 96
Harpeeh, Roddolph 18

Healthy Brew 124, 162
Heutel, Joseph 81, 82, 83, 84
Hoffbrau Steaks and Brewery 102, 111, 160, 161
homebrewing
  legalization 96, 159
  reference 171
Horn, Cam 121
House, Richard 96
Hubcap Brewery and Kitchen 102, 110, 160, 161
Hudec, James 114
Huerter, Andrew (Drew) 131, 148
Hughes, Steve 105
Hulsey, Aric 139
Humble, Gary 145
Humperdinks of Texas 112, 162
Humperdinks Restaurant and Brewery 112, 161, 162, 168
  Addison 104
  Arlington 103, 160
  Dallas 103, 104, 153, 161
  Irving 104
  Richardson 103, 160
Hunt, Jeremy 131
Huvelle, C.H. 43, 157

I

Independent Ale Works 163
Ireland, Darryl 104
Irving, TX 104, 153

J

Janik, Thomas 103, 153
Jetzer, Francisca. *See* Meisterhans, Francisca
Jogel, William 27
Jones, Austin 134
Jones, Kelly 102
Justin, TX 145

INDEX

K

Keeley Brewing Company of Texas 71
Keeley, Michael 36
Keeley, Thomas F. 37, 38, 67
Keller, TX 152
Kinchen, Al 103
Klein, Samuel 27, 37
Klein & Wolff 27
Kraft, Mike 102
Krum, TX 150
Kruse, Charles F. 78

L

Lakewood Brewing Company 133, 152, 163, 167
Lamsens, Orlando 73
Lamsens, Oscar 72, 73, 74, 76
Leftwich, Greg 139
legal disputes 35, 36, 46, 73, 79
legislation
  anti-trust laws 46
  earliest 55
  schoolhouse prohibition 56
  state 129, 141, 160
  Sunday "blue" laws 29
Leiter, Sam 72, 78, 79
Lemp, William J. 47
Lewis, Damon 134
Lewisville, TX 148
light beer 90, 91, 111, 159
Liotta, Dean 102
Little Elm, TX 150
local option
  after Prohibition 71, 85, 88, 129, 131
  before Prohibition 56, 57, 58, 60, 61, 64
  first election 57
Loeffler, Rusty 102
Lopez, Gary 111
Lyon, Jason 114

M

Maas, Henry K. 71, 85
Main Street Brewing Company 106, 160
March, Ken 124
Martin, Cody 141
Martin House Brewing Company 141, 163, 167
Mayer & Bruce 30, 43, 157
Mayer, Simon 21, 28, 29, 30, 155, 156, 157
McCarthy, J.C. 38
McFaddin, Lance 107
McKinney, TX 121
McMurray, John 103
Meisterhans, Charles 26, 27, 28, 29, 30, 33, 47, 156
Meisterhans, Francisca 26, 27, 33, 155
Mesberg, Harold W. 81, 82
Meyer, S. 27, 156
microbrewing 93
Miller Brewing Company 89, 90, 91, 92, 158, 159, 160, 168
Mingus Brewing Company 43, 157
Modano, Mike 146
Monduel, Jean 17, 18, 19, 155
Moon Under Water 95, 105, 160
Morgan, Samuel T. 61, 66, 67
Morrison, Johnny 102
Morriss, Matt 145
Mueller, August 19
Mullins, Bobby 141
Mycoskie, Craig 121
Myers, Adam 141

N

903 Brewers 141, 163, 167
non-alcoholic beer 99

O

O'Brien, Toby 101, 110
Oliphant, John 102
organic certification 124

Index

Orrell, Caton 145
Otto, Lee J. 79

P

Palo Pinto County, TX 43
Panther City Brewery and Café 104, 160
Pastrana, Alex 110
Perkinson, Brad 134
Peticolas Brewing Company 133, 162, 167
Peticolas, Michael 133
Piel, Jim 131
Plano, TX 93, 127
Porcari, Steve 139
Poynter, Jim 102
Prohibition
  federal 66, 67, 69
  repeal 70
  state 57, 59, 60, 61, 63, 66, 70
Pulver, Trevor 133

R

Rabbit Hole Brewing Company 145, 163, 167
Rahr, Frederick "Fritz" 113, 114, 116, 118
Rahr & Sons Brewing Company 113, 114, 116, 118, 120, 121, 133, 134, 147, 162, 167
railroads 25, 41, 54
Reardon, John 131
regulation
  city 139
  earliest 55
  federal 82
  state 62, 70, 96, 127
Reinheitsgebot Brewing Company 93, 94, 159
Revolver Brewing Company 139, 163, 167
Richardson, TX 103, 150
Richland Beverage Corp 99, 159
Roberts, Jeremy 141

Roberts, Natalie 141
Rock Bottom Brewing 102, 107, 160, 161
Rockwall County, TX 150
Ross, Robert 102
Routh Street Brewery and Grille 102, 110, 160, 161
Rowlett, TX 134

S

Saint Arnold Brewing Company 112
Sandidge, Steven 102, 107, 111
Schepps Brewing Corporation 76, 77, 80, 158
Schepps, George 75, 76, 77, 78, 80
Schepps, Julius 75, 76, 78, 84
Schepps, Phil 76, 77, 78
Schmidt, Gustav H. 27
Schooner Brewery 110, 161
Secchi, Gavin 114, 116, 121, 147
Seven Points, TX 134
Sharff, Aaron 104
Sherman, TX 141
Sims, John 104, 139
Slater, Gord 96
Spillers, Matt 133
St. Andrews Brewing Company 106, 160
Superior Brewing Company 71, 73, 74, 76, 78, 158
Swiss influence 27, 28

T

taprooms 141
taxation (alcohol)
  Baskin-McGregor Act 61, 62
  federal 19, 22, 85
  occupation tax (Civil War) 19, 22, 27, 33
  state 62
temperance movement 34, 35, 53, 55, 57, 58, 87, 89
Terry, Nathaniel 21, 155
Texas Association of Small Brewers 98

INDEX

Texas Beer Company 111, 152, 161
Texas Brewers Association 60
Texas Brewing Company (1891) 38, 43, 45, 46, 47, 48, 60, 64, 66, 67, 72, 157, 159
Texas Brewing Company (1993) 98, 99, 160, 161
Texas Select Beverage Company 99
Thompson, Don 93, 94, 95, 98, 105
Thompson, Mary 93, 94, 98, 105
Time Brewing Incorporated 80, 158
Tolbert, Kenny 102
Tucker, Davis 94, 95, 105
TwoRows Restaurant and Brewery
   Addison 112, 121, 162
   Dallas 102, 160, 162

U

Uncle Buck's Brewery and Steakhouse 125, 162, 169
Union Bear 133, 139, 163, 169
USA Café (USA Brewing Company) 107, 110, 161

V

Volstead Act (1919) 66, 69

W

Wagenhauser, Anton 33, 35, 36, 156, 157
Wagenhauser Brewing Association 33, 35, 36, 156
water quality 38, 47
Weatherford, TX 21, 33
Wedemeier, Dave 141
Wehrmann, Dennis 121, 123
West End Brewing Company 96, 159
W.F. Both & Co. 21, 33, 156
Wheeler (first name unknown) 18, 19, 155
Willard, Frances E. 58, 59
Williams, Jeff 105
Wisniewski, Jim 106
Wood, Grant 139
World War I 65
World War II 76, 82, 83, 84
Wulfert, Fritz 22
Wynne, Shannon 106, 148

Y

Yegua Creek Brewing Company 101, 110, 160, 161
Younge, James 57

Z

Zane-Cetti, Jesse Shenton 25, 38, 41, 48, 64, 67
Zelzer, Manny 99
Zimmerman, Herman 48
Zio Carlo Magnolia Brew Pub 134, 162, 169

ABOUT THE AUTHORS

Paul Hightower wears many hats. Educated as a research scientist and with a former career as an IT consultant, he now works as a freelance writer and editor for science, technology and educational topics. Hightower also has a keen interest in modern craft beer and the Texas brewing industry, with previous publications on Texas craft beer and breweries, and he has been writing as the Dallas Craft Beer Examiner since 2009. He is a BJCP certified beer judge as well as a reasonable homebrewer.

Brian Brown first discovered his passion for craft beer after trying a German-style hefeweizen in the late 1990s. Since then, he has spent countless hours studying the history and science of beer, which led him to become a certified judge through the BJCP. In the summer of 2010, he began writing for Examiner.com under the title of Plano Craft Beer Examiner, and in 2013, he founded the website BeerInBigD.com. Born in Dallas, he now lives north of the city with his wife and their two children.

Visit us at
www.historypress.net

This title is also available as an e-book

www.ingramcontent.com/pod-product-compliance
Lightning Source LLC
Chambersburg PA
CBHW070345100426
42812CB00005B/1429